Machine Habitus

Machine Habitus

Toward a Sociology of Algorithms

Massimo Airoldi

polity

First published in 2022 by Polity Press

Polity Press
65 Bridge Street
Cambridge CB2 1UR, UK

Polity Press
101 Station Landing
Suite 300
Medford, MA 02155, USA

ISBN-13: 978-1-5095-4327-4
ISBN-13: 978-1-5095-4328-1 (pb)

A catalogue record for this book is available from the British Library.

Library of Congress Control Number: 2021939495

Typeset in 10.5 on 12 pt Sabon
by Fakenham Prepress Solutions, Fakenham, Norfolk NR21 8NL
Printed and bound in Great Britain by CPI Group (UK) Ltd, Croydon

The publisher has used its best endeavours to ensure that the URLs for external websites referred to in this book are correct and active at the time of going to press. However, the publisher has no responsibility for the websites and can make no guarantee that a site will remain live or that the content is or will remain appropriate.

Every effort has been made to trace all copyright holders, but if any have been overlooked the publisher will be pleased to include any necessary credits in any subsequent reprint or edition.

For further information on Polity, visit our website:
politybooks.com

Contents

Habitus, c'est un grand mot pour dire quelque chose, je crois, de très complexe. C'est à dire, une espèce de petite machine génératrice – pour une analogie un peu sauvage, un programme d'ordinateur – à partir duquel les gens engendrent des foules des réponses à des foules des situations.

Pierre Bourdieu
Interview with Antoine Spire, 1990

If social order is made of propensities to associate, if to be social is a propensity to associate, then big data conversion events operationalize association in matrices of propensity.

Adrian Mackenzie, 2018

Acknowledgements

I would like to thank Salvatore Iaconesi and Oriana Persico for taking part in two interview sessions, in the autumn of 2019 and the summer of 2020, and being a unique source of inspiration. I must also thank Hanan Salam, founder of Women in AI, for her technical clarifications and preliminary comments on this book project, and Debora Pizzimenti, for providing me with further details about the IAQOS experience. A big thanks to Alessandro Gandini, Mauro Barisione, Adam Arvidsson, and Polity's editors and anonymous reviewers, for their insightful comments and encouragement all the way through. I also thank all my colleagues and students at EM Lyon. Last, a huge thanks to Stefania, my most important person.

Figures and Tables

Figures

Tables

Preface

On 31 March 2019, a new member of the multicultural community of Torpignattara, a semi-peripheral district of the city of Rome, was born. The event was greeted with unprecedented excitement in the neighbourhood, culminating, on the big day, with a small welcome party of friends and curious others who had gathered to support Salvatore and Oriana. Over the previous weeks, everybody had left a message, a wish or even a drawing, in paper boxes distributed for the occasion across the shops and bars of Torpignattara. The neighbourhood became an extended family to the long-awaited newcomer, who was only few days old when it got to know everyone, rolling from door to door in the stroller, and passing from hand to hand. Whether at the local café, or on the way to the drug store, there was always someone with a story to tell – usually about the local community and its history, places, people, food, hopes and fears. The baby listened, and learned. Soon, like any other child in Torpignattara, it would go to the Carlo Pisacane elementary school just around the corner. But IAQOS – that's its name – was certainly not like other babies. It was the first 'open-source neighbourhood AI', developed by the artist and robotic engineer Salvatore Iaconesi together with the artist and communication scientist Oriana Persico, in a collaboration funded by the Italian government and involving several cultural and research institutions.

In concrete terms, IAQOS is a relatively simple software agent that can communicate through a tablet or a computer via natural language, recognizing the voices and gestures of its interlocutors and learning from them. Differently from the algorithmic systems we encounter every day through our devices – such as those running in Google Search, Facebook, Amazon, Instagram, Netflix or YouTube – this open-source art project had no other goal than accumulating social data about the neighbourhood, behaving as a sort of 'baby AI'. Like a real baby, it observed the surrounding social environment, absorbed a contextual worldview and used the acquired knowledge to successfully participate in social life. By doing all that, during the spring of 2019, IAQOS became in effect a 'fijo de Torpigna'; that is, an artificial yet authentic member of the local community, sharing a common imaginary, vocabulary and social background, and capable of building social relations (Iaconesi and Persico 2019).

This peculiar example makes it easier to see what many sociologists and social scientists have so far overlooked: the fact that a machine which learns from patterns in human-generated data, and autonomously manipulates human language, knowledge and relations, is more than a machine. It is a *social agent*: a participant in society, simultaneously participated in by it. As such, it becomes a legitimate object of sociological research.

We already know that algorithms are instruments of power, that they play with the lives of people and communities in opaque ways and at different scales, deciding who will be eligible or not for a loan with the same statistical nonchalance with which they move emails to the junk folder. We know that filter bubbles threaten to draw digital boundaries among voters and consumers, and that autonomous robots can be trained to kill. Moreover, we know that some algorithms can learn from us. They can learn how to speak like humans, how to write like philosophers, how to recommend songs like music experts. And they can learn how to be sexist like a conservative man, racist like a white supremacist, classist like an elitist snob. In sum, it is increasingly evident how similar we – humans and machines – have become. However, perhaps because comparisons and analyses have mostly been limited to examining cognition, abilities and biases, we have somehow failed to see the socio-logical reason for this similarity: that is, culture.

This book identifies culture as the seed transforming machines into social agents. Since the term is 'one of the two or three most complicated words in the English language' (Williams 1983: 87), let me clarify: here I use 'culture' to refer essentially to practices, classifications, tacit norms and dispositions associated with specific positions in society. Culture is more than data: it is relational patterns in the data. As such, culture operates in the code of machine learning systems, tacitly orienting their predictions. It works as a set of statistical dispositions rooted in a datafied social environment – like a social media feed, or like IAQOS' multi-cultural neighbourhood.

The culture in the code allows machine learning algorithms to deal with the complexity of our social realities as if they truly understood meaning, or were somehow socialized. Learning machines can make a difference in the social world, and recursively adapt to its variations. As Salvatore Iaconesi and Oriana Persico noted in one of our interviews: 'IAQOS exists, and this existence allows other people to modify themselves, as well as modify IAQOS.' The code is in the culture too, and confounds it through techno-social interactions and algorithmic distinctions – between the relevant and the irrelevant, the similar and the different, the likely and the unlikely, the visible and the invisible. Hence, together with humans, machines actively contribute to the reproduction of the social order – that is, to the incessant drawing and redrawing of the social and symbolic bound-aries that objectively and intersubjectively divide society into different, unequally powerful portions.

As I write, a large proportion of the world's population has been advised or forced to stay home, due to the Covid-19 emergency. Face-to-face interactions have been reduced to a minimum, while our use of digital devices has reached a novel maximum. The new normal of digital isolation coincides with our increased production of data as workers, citizens and consumers, and the decrease of industrial production *strictu sensu*. Our social life is almost entirely mediated by digital infrastructures populated by learning machines and predictive technologies, incessantly processing traces of users' socially structured practices. It has never been so evident that studying how society unfolds requires us to treat algorithms as something more than cold mathematical objects. As Gillespie argues, 'a sociological analysis must not conceive of algorithms as abstract, technical achievements, but must unpack the warm human and institutional choices that lie behind these cold mechanisms' (2014: 169). This book sees culture as the warm human matter lying inside machine learning systems, and theorizes how to unpack it sociologically by means of the notion of *machine habitus*.

1

Why Not a Sociology of Algorithms?

Machines as sociological objects

Algorithms of various kinds hold the social world together. Financial transactions, dating, advertising, news circulation, work organization, policing tasks, music discovery, hiring processes, customer relations – all are to a large extent delegated to non-human agents embedded in digital infrastructures. For some years we have all been aware of this, thanks to academic research and popular books, journalistic reports and documentaries. Whether from the daily news headlines or the dystopian allegories of TV series, we have come to recognize that almost everything is now 'algorithmic' and that artificial intelligence is revolutionizing all aspects of human life (Amoore and Piotukh 2016). Even leaving aside the simplifications of popular media and the wishful thinking of techno-chauvinists, this is true for the most part (Broussard 2018; Sumpter 2018). Yet, many sociologists and social scientists continue to ignore algorithms and AI technologies in their research, or consider them at best a part of the supposedly inanimate material background of social life. When researchers study everyday life, consumption, social interactions, media, organizations, cultural taste or social representations, they often unknowingly observe the consequences of the opaque algorithmic processes at play in digital platforms and devices (Beer 2013a). In this book, I argue that it is time to see both people and intelligent machines as active agents in the ongoing realization of the social order, and I propose a set of conceptual tools for this purpose.

Why only now?, one may legitimately ask. In fact, the distinction between humans and machines has been a widely debated subject in the social sciences for decades (see Cerulo 2009; Fields 1987). Strands of sociological research such as Science and Technology Studies (STS) and Actor-Network Theory (ANT) have strongly questioned mainstream sociology's lack of attention to the technological and material aspects of social life.

In 1985, Steve Woolgar's article 'Why Not a Sociology of Machines?' appeared in the British journal *Sociology*. Its main thesis was that, just as a 'sociology of science' had appeared problematic before Kuhn's theory of scientific paradigms but was later turned into an established field of research, intelligent machines should finally become 'legitimate sociological objects' (Woolgar 1985: 558). More than thirty-five years later, this is still a largely unaccomplished goal. When Woolgar's article was published, research on AI systems was heading for a period of stagnation commonly known as the 'AI winter', which lasted up until the recent and ongoing hype around big-data-powered AI (Floridi 2020). According to Woolgar, the main goal of a sociology of machines was to examine the practical day-to-day activities and discourses of AI researchers. Several STS scholars have subsequently followed this direction (e.g. Seaver 2017; Neyland 2019). However, Woolgar also envisioned an alternative sociology of machines with 'intelligent machines as the subjects of study', adding that 'this project will only strike us as bizarre to the extent that we are unwilling to grant human intelligence to intelligent machines' (1985: 567). This latter option may not sound particularly bizarre today, given that a large variety of tasks requiring human intelligence are now routinely accomplished by algorithmic systems, and that computer scientists propose to study the social behaviour of autonomous machines ethologically, as if they were animals in the wild (Rahwan et al. 2019).

Even when technological artefacts could hardly be considered 'intelligent',[1] actor-network theorists radically revised human-centric notions of agency by portraying both material objects and humans as 'actants', that is, as sources of action in networks of relations (Latour 2005; Akrich 1992; Law 1990). Based on this theoretical perspective, both a ringing doorbell and the author of this book can be seen as equally agentic (Cerulo 2009: 534). ANT strongly opposes not only the asymmetry between humans and machines, but also the more general ontological divide between the social and the natural, the animated and the material. This philosophical position has encountered a diffuse criticism (Cerulo 2009: 535; Müller 2015: 30), since it is hardly compatible with most of the anthropocentric theories employed in sociology – except for that of Gabriel Tarde (Latour et al. 2012). Still, one key intuition of ANT increasingly resonates throughout the social sciences, as well as in the present work: that what we call social life is nothing but the socio-material product of heterogeneous arrays of relations, involving human as well as non-human agents.

According to ANT scholar John Law (1990: 8), a divide characterized sociological research at the beginning of the 1990s. On the one hand, the majority of researchers were concerned with 'the social', and thus studying canonical topics such as inequalities, culture and power by focusing exclusively on people. On the other hand, a minority of sociologists were studying the 'merely technical' level of machines, in fields like STS or ANT. They examined the micro-relations between scientists and laboratory equipment (Latour and Woolgar 1986), or the techno-social making of aeroplanes and gyroscopes (MacKenzie 1996), without taking part to the 'old' sociological debates about social structures and political struggles (MacKenzie and Wajcman 1999: 19). It can be argued that the divide described by Law still persists today in sociology, although it has become evident that 'the social

---

[1] The status of artificial intelligence – whether it could ever become 'general', or is destined to remain a 'narrow' mathematical manifestation as in the case of current machine learning systems – is a debated issue that goes beyond the scope of the present work. For a non-technical overview, see Broussard 2018.

order is not a social order at all. Rather it is a *sociotechnical order*. What appears to be social is partly technical. What we usually call technical is partly social' (Law 1990: 10).

With the recent emergence of a multidisciplinary scholarship on the biases and discriminations of algorithmic systems, the interplay between 'the social' and 'the technical' has become more visible than in the past. One example is the recent book by the information science scholar Safiya Umoja Noble, *Algorithms of Oppression* (2018), which illustrates how Google Search results tend to reproduce racial and gender stereotypes. Far from being 'merely technical' and, therefore, allegedly neutral, the unstable socio-technical arrangement of algorithmic systems, web content, content providers and crowds of googling users on the platform contributes to the discriminatory social representations of African Americans. According to Noble, more than neutrally mirroring the unequal culture of the United States as a historically divided country, the (socio-)technical arrangement of Google Search amplifies and reifies the commodification of black women's bodies.

I believe that it should be sociology's job to explain and theorize why and under what circumstances algorithmic systems may behave this way. The theoretical toolkit of ethology mobilized by Rahwan and colleagues (2019) in a recent *Nature* article is probably not up to this aim, for a quite simple reason: machine learning tools are eminently *social* animals. They learn from the social – datafied, quantified and transformed into computationally processable information – and then they manipulate it, by drawing probabilistic relations among people, objects and information. While Rahwan et al. are right in putting forward the 'scientific study of intelligent machines, not as engineering artefacts, but as a class of actors with particular behavioural patterns and ecology' (2019: 477), their analytical framework focuses on 'evolutionary' and 'environmental' dimensions only, downplaying the cornerstone of anthropological and sociological explanations, that is, culture. Here I argue that, in order to understand the causes and implications of algorithmic behaviour, it is necessary to first comprehend how culture enters the code of algorithmic systems, and how it is shaped by algorithms in turn.

Two major technological and social transformations that have taken place over the past decade make the need for a sociology of algorithms particularly pressing. A first, *quantitative* shift has resulted from the unprecedented penetration of digital technologies into the lives and routines of people and organizations. The rapid diffusion of smartphones since the beginning of the 2010s has literally put powerful computers in the hands of billions of individuals throughout the world, including in its poorest and most isolated regions (IWS 2020). Today's global economic system relies on algorithms, data and networked infrastructures to the point that fibre Internet connections are no longer fast enough for automated financial transactions, leading to faster microwave or laser-based communication systems being installed on rooftops near New York's trading centres in order to speed up algorithmic exchanges (D. MacKenzie 2018). Following the physical distancing norms imposed worldwide during the Covid-19 pandemic, the human reliance on digital technologies for work, leisure and interpersonal communication appears to have increased even further. Most of the world's population now participates in what can be alternatively labelled 'platform society' (van Dijck, Poell and de Waal 2018), 'metadata society' (Pasquinelli 2018) or 'surveillance capitalism' (Zuboff 2019), that is, socio-economic systems heavily dependent on the massive extraction and predictive analysis of data. There have never been so many machines so deeply embedded in the heterogeneous bundle of culture, relations, institutions and practices that sociologists call 'society'.

A second, *qualitative* shift concerns the types of machines and AI technologies embedded in our digital society. The development and industrial implementation of machine learning algorithms that 'enable computers to learn from experience' have marked an important turning point. 'Experience', in this context, is essentially 'a dataset of historic events', and 'learning' means 'identifying and extracting useful patterns from a dataset' (Kelleher 2019: 253).

In 1989, Lenat noted in the pages of the journal *Machine Learning* that 'human-scale learning demands a human-scale amount of knowledge' (1989: 255), which was not yet available to AI researchers at the time. An impressive advancement of machine learning methods occurred two decades later, thanks to a 'fundamental socio-technological transformation of the relationship between humans and machines', consisting in the capturing of human cognitive abilities through the digital accumulation of data (Mühlhoff 2020: 1868). This paradigmatic change has made the ubiquitous automation of social and cultural tasks suddenly possible on an unprecedented scale. What matters here sociologically is 'not what happens in the machine's artificial brain, but what the machine tells its users and the consequences of this' (Esposito 2017: 250). According to Esposito, thanks to the novel cultural and communicative capabilities developed by 'parasitically' taking advantage of human-generated online data, algorithms have substantially turned into 'social agents'.

Recent accomplishments in AI research – such as AlphaGo, the deep learning system that achieved a historic win against the world champion of the board game Go in 2016 (Chen 2016; Broussard 2018), or GPT-3, a powerful algorithmic model released in 2020, capable of autonomously writing poems, computer code and even philosophical texts (Weinberg 2020; Askell 2020) – indicate that the ongoing shift toward the increasingly active and autonomous participation of algorithmic systems in the social world is likely to continue into the near future. But let's have a look at the past first.

Algorithms and their applications, from Euclid to AlphaGo

The term 'algorithm' is believed to derive from the French bastardization of the name of the ninth-century Persian mathematician al-Khwārizmī, the author of the oldest known work of algebra. Being originally employed in medieval Western Europe to indicate the novel calculation methods alternative to those based on Roman numerals, in more recent times the term has come to mean 'any process of systematic calculation [...] that could be carried out automatically' (Chabert 1999: 2). As Chabert remarks in his book *A History of the Algorithm*: 'algorithms have been around since the beginning of time and existed well before a special word had been coined to describe them' (1999: 1). Euclid's algorithm for determining the greatest common divisor of two integers, known since the fourth century BCE, is one of the earliest examples.

More generally, algorithms can be intended as computational recipes, that is, step-by-step instructions for transforming input data into a desired output (Gillespie 2014). According to Gillespie (2016: 19), algorithms are essentially operationalized procedures that must be distinguished from both their underlying 'model' – the 'formalization of a problem and its goal, articulated in computational terms' – and their final context of application, such as the technical infrastructure of a social media platform like Facebook, where sets of algorithms are used to allocate personalized content and ads in users' feeds. Using a gastronomic metaphor, the step-by-step procedure for cooking an apple pie is the algorithm, the cookbook recipe works as the model, and the kitchen represents the application context. However, in current public and academic discourse, these different components and meanings tend to be conflated, and the term algorithm is broadly employed as a synecdoche for a 'complex socio-technical assemblage' (Gillespie 2016: 22).

'Algorithm' is thus a slippery umbrella term, which may refer to different things (Seaver 2017). There are many kinds of computational recipes, which vary based on their realms of application as well as on the specific 'algorithmic techniques' employed to order information and process data (Rieder 2020). A single task, such as classifying texts by topic, may concern domains as diverse as email 'spam' filtering, online content moderation, product recommendation, behavioural targeting, credit scoring, financial trading and more – all of which involve a plethora of possible input data and outputs. Furthermore, text classification tasks can be executed in several – yet all 'algorithmic' – ways: by hand, with pen and paper only; through *rule-following* software applying models predefined by human programmers (e.g. counting topic-related word occurrences within texts); or via 'intelligent' *machine learning* systems that are not explicitly programmed a priori. These latter can be either *supervised* – i.e. requiring a preliminary training process based on data examples, as in the case of naive Bayes text classifiers (Rieder

2017) – or *unsupervised*, that is, machine learning techniques working without pre-assigned outputs, like Latent Dirichlet Allocation in the field of topic modeling (Bechmann and Bowker 2019).

This book does not aim to offer heavily technical definitions, nor an introduction to algorithm design and AI technologies; the reader can easily find such notions elsewhere.[2] Throughout the text, I will frequently make use of the generic terms 'algorithm' and 'machine' to broadly indicate automated systems producing outputs based on the computational elaboration of input data. However, in order to highlight the sociological relevance of the quali-quantitative transition from Euclid's calculations to today's seemingly 'intelligent' artificial agents like GPT-3 and AlphaGo, some preliminary conceptual distinctions are needed. It is apparent, in fact, that the everyday socio-cultural implications of algebraic formulas solved for centuries by hand or via mechanical calculators are not even close in magnitude to those of the algorithms currently governing information networks.

Below I briefly outline the history of algorithms and their applications – from ancient algebra to rule-following models running on digital computers, and beyond to platform-based machine learning systems. This socio-technical evolution can be roughly broken into three main *eras*, visually summarized in Figure 1 at the end of this section. Without pretending to be exhaustive, the proposed periodization focuses especially on the emergence of 'public relevance algorithms' (Gillespie 2014: 168), that is, automated systems dealing with the social matter of human knowledge, experience and practice.

Analogue Era (–1945)
Taking analogue to mean 'not-digital' (Sterne 2016), this first historical phase ranges in principle from the invention

---

[2] For an overview of AI systems and deep learning methods, see Kelleher 2019. For an introduction to music recommenders, see Celma 2010. Historical accounts and non-technical explanations of machine learning systems can be found in Pasquinelli 2017; Broussard 2018; Sumpter 2018; Natale and Ballatore 2020; and Mackenzie 2015.

and manual application of algorithms by ancient mathematicians to the realization of the first digital computers right after the Second World War. Within this period, algorithms were applied either by human-supervised mechanical devices or by humans themselves (Pasquinelli 2017). In fact, up until the early twentieth century, the word 'computer' indicated a person employed to make calculations by hand. Mechanical computers started to be conceptualized at the beginning of the nineteenth century, following Leibniz's early intuitions about the mechanization of calculus (Chabert 1999), as well as a rising demand for faster and more reliable calculations from companies and governments (Wilson 2018; Campbell-Kelly et al. 2013). Aiming to automatize the compilation of tables for navigation at sea, particularly strategic for the British Empire, in the 1820s the mathematician Charles Babbage designed the first mechanical computer, the Difference Engine, which was then followed by the more ambitious Analytical Engine – ideally capable of performing 'any calculation that a human could specify for it' (Campbell-Kelly et al. 2013: 8). Babbage's proto-computers were pioneering scientific projects that remained largely on paper, but more concrete applications of simpler electro-mechanical 'algorithm machines' (Gillespie 2014) came to light by the end of the century. In 1890, Hollerith's electric tabulating system was successfully employed to process US census data, paving the way for the foundation of IBM. Thanks to the punched-card machines designed by Hollerith, information on over 62 million American citizens was processed within 'only' two and a half years, compared with the seven years taken by the previous census, with an estimated saving of 5 million dollars (Campbell-Kelly et al. 2013: 17–18). The mass production of desk calculators and business accounting machines brought algorithms closer to ordinary people's everyday routines. Still, information was computationally transformed and elaborated solely through analogue means (e.g. punched cards, paper tapes) and under human supervision.

Digital Era (1946–1998)
Through the 1930s and the 1940s, a number of theoretical and technological advances in the computation of

information took place, accelerated by the war and its scientific needs (Wiener 1989). The Harvard Mark I became the 'first fully automatic machine to be completed', in 1943. However, it was still 'programmed by a length of paper tape some three inches wide on which "operation codes" were punched' (Campbell-Kelly et al. 2013: 57). The pathbreaking conceptual work of the British mathematician Alan Turing was crucial to the development of the first modern electronic computer, known as ENIAC, in 1946. It was a thousand times faster than the Harvard Mark I, and finally capable of holding 'both the instructions of a program and the numbers on which it operated' (Campbell-Kelly et al. 2013: 76). For the first time, it was possible to design algorithmic models, run them, read input data and write output results all in digital form, as combinations of binary numbers stored as bits. This digital shift produced a significant jump in data processing speed and power, previously limited by physical constraints. Algorithms became inextricably linked to a novel discipline called computer science (Chabert 1999).

With supercomputers making their appearance in companies and universities, the automated processing of information became increasingly embedded into the mechanisms of post-war capitalism. Finance was one of the first civil industries to systematically exploit technological innovations in computing and telecommunications, as in the case of the London Stock Exchange described by Pardo-Guerra (2010). From 1955 onwards, the introduction of mechanical and digital technologies transformed financial trading into a mainly automated practice, sharply different from 'face-to-face dealings on the floor', which had been the norm up to that point.

In these years, the ancient dream of creating 'thinking machines' was spread among a new generation of scientists, often affiliated to the MIT lab led by professor Marvin Minsky, known as the 'father' of AI research (Natale and Ballatore 2020). Since the 1940s, the cross-disciplinary field of cybernetics had been working on the revolutionary idea that machines could autonomously interact with their environment and learn from it through feedback mechanisms (Wiener 1989). In 1957, the cognitive scientist Frank

Rosenblatt designed and built a cybernetic machine called Perceptron, the first operative artificial neural network, assembled as an analogue algorithmic system made of input sensors and resolved into one single dichotomic output – a light bulb that could be on or off, depending on the computational result (Pasquinelli 2017). Rosenblatt's bottom-up approach to artificial cognition did not catch on in AI research. An alternative top-down approach, now known as 'symbolic AI' or 'GOFAI' (Good Old-Fashioned Artificial Intelligence), dominated the field in the following decades, up until the boom of machine learning. The 'intelligence' of GOFAI systems was formulated as a set of predetermined instructions capable of 'simulating' human cognitive performance – for instance by effectively playing chess (Fjelland 2020). Such a deductive, rule-based logic (Pasquinelli 2017) rests at the core of software programming, as exemplified by the conditional IF–THEN commands running in the back end of any computer application.

From the late 1970s, the development of microprocessors and the subsequent commercialization of personal computers fostered the popularization of computer programming. By entering people's lives at work and at home – e.g. with videogames, word processors, statistical software, etc. – computer algorithms were no longer the reserve of a few scientists working for governments, large companies and universities (Campbell-Kelly et al. 2013). The digital storage of information, as well as its grassroots creation and circulation through novel Internet-based channels (e.g. emails, Internet Relay Chats, discussion forums), translated into the availability of novel data sources. The automated processing of large volumes of such 'user-generated data' for commercial purposes, inaugurated by the development of the Google search engine in the late 1990s, marked the transition toward a third era of algorithmic applications.

Platform Era (1998–)
The global Internet-based information system known as the World Wide Web was invented in 1989, and the first browser for web navigation was released to the general public two years later. Soon, the rapid multiplication of web content led to a pressing need for indexing solutions capable of

overcoming the growing 'information overload' experienced by Internet users (Benkler 2006; Konstan and Riedl 2012). In 1998, Larry Page and Sergey Brin designed an algorithm able to 'find needles in haystacks', which then became the famous PageRank of Google Search (MacCormick 2012: 25). Building on graph theory and citation analysis, this algorithm measured the hierarchical relations among web pages based on hyperlinks. 'Bringing order to the web' through the data-driven identification of 'important' search results was the main goal of Page and colleagues (1999). With the implementation of PageRank, 'the web is no longer treated exclusively as a document repository, but additionally as a social system' (Rieder 2020: 285). Unsupervised algorithms, embedded in the increasingly modular and dynamic infrastructure of web services, started to be developed by computer scientists to automatically process, quantify and classify the social web (Beer 2009). As it became possible to extract and organize in large databases the data produced in real time by millions of consumers, new forms of Internet-based surveillance appeared (Arvidsson 2004; Zwick and Denegri Knott 2009). The development of the first automated recommender systems in the early 1990s led a few years later to a revolution in marketing and e-commerce (Konstan and Riedl 2012). Personalized recommendations aimed to predict consumer desires and assist purchasing choices (Ansari, Essegaier and Kohli 2000), with businesses being offered the promise of keeping their customers 'forever' (Pine II, Peppers and Rogers 1995). The modular socio-technical infrastructures of commercial platforms such as Google, Amazon and, beginning in the mid 2000s, YouTube, Facebook and Twitter, lie at the core of this historical transition toward the datafication and algorithmic ordering of economy and society (Mayer-Schoenberger and Cukier 2013; van Dijck 2013; Zuboff 2019).

Digital platforms are at once the main context of application of these autonomous machines and the ultimate source of their intelligence. Platformization has been identified as one of the causes of the current 'eternal spring' of AI research, since it has finally provided the enormous amount of data and real-time feedback needed to train machine learning models, such as users' profile pictures, online transactions or social media posts (Helmond 2015). Together with the development of faster and higher performing computers, this access to 'big' and relatively inexpensive data made possible the breakthrough of 'deep learning' in the 2010s (Kelleher 2019). As Mühlhoff notes (2020: 1869), most industrial AI implementations 'come with extensive media infrastructure for capturing humans in distributed, human-machine computing networks, which as a whole perform the intelligence capacity that is commonly attributed to the computer system'. Hence, it is not by chance that the top players in the Internet industry, in the US as in China, have taken the lead of the AI race. In 2016, Joaquin Candela, director of the Facebook Applied Machine Learning Group, declared: 'we're trying to build more than 1.5 billion AI agents – one for every person who uses Facebook or any of its products' (Higginbotham 2016, cited in A. Mackenzie 2019: 1995).

Furthermore, while in the Digital Era algorithms were commercially used mainly for analytical purposes, in the Platform Era they also became 'operational' devices (A. Mackenzie 2018). Logistic regressions such as those run in SPSS by statisticians in the 1980s could now be operationally embedded in a platform infrastructure and fed with thousands of data 'features' in order to autonomously filter the content presented to single users based on adaptable, high-dimensional models (Rieder 2020). The computational implications of this shift have been described by Adrian Mackenzie as follows:

> if conventional statistical regression models typically worked with 10 different variables [...] and perhaps sample sizes of thousands, data mining and predictive analytics today typically work with hundreds and in some cases tens of thousands of variables and sample sizes of millions or billions. The difference between classical statistics, which often sought to explain associations between variables, and machine learning, which seeks to explore high-dimensional patterns, arises because vector spaces juxtapose almost any number of features. (Mackenzie 2015: 434)

Advanced AI models built using artificial neural networks are now used in chatbots, self-driving cars and recommendation systems, and have enabled the recent expansion of

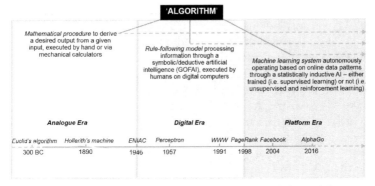

Figure 1 Algorithms: a conceptual map, from Euclid to AlphaGo

fields such as pattern recognition, machine translation or image generation. In 2015, an AI system developed by the Google-owned company DeepMind was the first to win against a professional player at the complex game of Go. On the one hand, this landmark was a matter of increased computing power.[3] On the other hand, it was possible thanks to the aforementioned qualitative shift from a top-down artificial reasoning based on 'symbolic deduction' to a bottom-up 'statistical induction' (Pasquinelli 2017). AlphaGo – the machine's name – learned how to play the ancient board game largely on its own, by 'attempting to match the moves of expert players from recorded games' (Chen 2016: 6). Far from mechanically executing tasks, current AI technologies can learn from (datafied) experience, a bit like human babies. And as with human babies, once thrown into the world, these machine learning systems are no less than social agents, who shape society and are shaped by it in turn.

[3] Chen writes: 'in 1983, CPU speed or frequency was 25 MHz. Assuming 1,000 CPU cycles correspond to making a decision on a Go board, it would have taken 31 minutes to make a decision about $361 \times 360 \times 359 = 46,655,640$ possible moves back then. Today, a single CPU's frequency is above 4 GHz, [...] making it 160 times faster on the same algorithm – in this case, taking less than 12 seconds to make that same decision' (2016: 6).

Critical algorithm studies

When algorithms started to be applied to the digital engineering of the social world, only a few sociologists took notice (Orton-Johnson and Prior 2013). In the early 2000s, the sociological hype about the (then new) social networking sites, streaming platforms and dating services was largely about the possible emancipatory outcomes of an enlarged digital connectivity, the disrupting research potential of big data, and the narrowing divide between 'real' and 'virtual' lives (Beer 2009). However, at the periphery of academic sociology, social scientists working in fields like software studies, anthropology, philosophy, cultural studies, geography, Internet studies and media research were beginning to theorize and investigate the emergence of a new 'algorithmic life' (Amoore and Piotukh 2016). In the past decade, this research strand has grown substantially, disrupting disciplinary borders and setting the agenda of important academic outlets.[4] Known as 'critical algorithm studies' (Gillespie and Seaver 2016), it proposes multiple *sociologies of algorithms* which tackle various aspects of the techno-social data assemblages behind AI technologies.

A major part of this critical literature has scrutinized the production of the *input* of automated calculations, that is, the data. Critical research on the mining of data through digital forms of surveillance (Brayne 2017; van Dijck 2013) and labour (Casilli 2019; Gandini 2020) has illuminated the extractive and 'panopticist' character of platforms, Internet services and connected devices such as wearables and smart-phones (see Lupton 2020; Ruckenstein and Granroth 2020; Arvidsson 2004). Cheney-Lippold (2011, 2017) developed the notion of 'algorithmic identity' in order to study the biopolitical implications of web analytics firms' data harnessing, aimed at computationally predicting who digital consumers

---

[4] Since 2015, special issues on the critical study of algorithms have appeared in recognized social science journals such as the *European Journal of Cultural Studies, Information, Communication & Society, New Media & Society, Technology & Human Values, Theory, Culture & Society*, and more.

are. Similar studies have also been conducted in the field of critical marketing (Cluley and Brown 2015; Darmody and Zwick 2020; Zwick and Denegri-Knott 2009). Furthermore, a number of works have questioned the epistemological grounds of 'big data' approaches, highlighting how the automated and decontextualized analysis of large datasets may ultimately lead to inaccurate or biased results (boyd and Crawford 2012; O'Neil 2016; Broussard 2018). The proliferation of metrics and the ubiquity of 'datafication' – that is, the transformation of social action into online quantified data (Mayer-Schoenberger and Cukier 2013) – have been indicated as key features of today's capitalism, which is seen as increasingly dependent on the harvesting and engineering of consumers' lives and culture (Zuboff 2019; van Dijck, Poell and de Waal 2018).

As STS research did decades earlier with missiles and electric bulbs (MacKenzie and Wajcman 1999), critical algorithm studies have also explored how algorithmic models and their data infrastructures are developed, manufactured and narrated, eventually with the aim of making these opaque 'black boxes' accountable (Pasquale 2015). The 'anatomy' of AI systems is the subject of the original work of Crawford and Joler (2018), at the crossroads of art and research. Taking Amazon Echo – the consumer voice-enabled AI device featuring the popular interface Alexa – as an example, the authors show how even the most banal human–device interaction 'requires a vast planetary network, fueled by the extraction of non-renewable materials, labor, and data' (Crawford and Joler 2018: 2). Behind the capacity of Amazon Echo to hear, interpret and efficiently respond to users' commands, there is not only a machine learning model in a constant process of optimization, but also a wide array of accumulated scientific knowledge, natural resources such as the lithium and cobalt used in batteries, and labour exploited in the mining of both rare metals and data. Several studies have looked more closely into the genesis of specific platforms and algorithmic systems, tracing their historical evolution and practical implementation while simultaneously unveiling the cultural and political assumptions inscribed in their technicalities (Rieder 2017; D. MacKenzie 2018; Helmond, Nieborg and van der Vlist 2019; Neyland 2019; Seaver

2019; Eubanks 2018; Hallinan and Striphas 2016; McKelvey 2018; Gillespie 2018). Furthermore, since algorithms are also cultural and discursive objects (Beer 2017; Seaver 2017; Bucher 2017; Campolo and Crawford 2020), researchers have investigated how they are marketed and – as often happens – mythicized (Natale and Ballatore 2020; Neyland 2019). This literature shows how the fictitious representation of calculative devices as necessarily neutral, objective and accurate in their predictions is ideologically rooted in the techno-chauvinistic belief that 'tech is always the solution' (Broussard 2018: 7).

A considerable amount of research has also asked how and to what extent the *output* of algorithmic computations – automated recommendations, micro-targeted ads, search results, risk predictions, etc. – controls and influences citizens, workers and consumers. Many critical scholars have argued that the widespread delegation of human choices to opaque algorithms results in a limitation of human freedom and agency (e.g. Pasquale 2015; Mackenzie 2006; Ananny 2016; Beer 2013a, 2017; Ziewitz 2016; Just and Latzer 2017). Building on the work of Lash (2007) and Thrift (2005), the sociologist David Beer (2009) suggested that online algorithms not only mediate but also 'constitute' reality, becoming a sort of 'technological unconscious', an invisible force orienting Internet users' everyday lives. Other contributions have similarly portrayed algorithms as powerful 'engines of order' (Rieder 2020), such as Taina Bucher's research on how Facebook 'programmes' social life (2012a, 2018). Scholars have examined the effects of algorithmic 'governance' (Ziewitz 2016) in a number of research contexts, by investigating computational forms of racial discrimination (Noble 2018; Benjamin 2019), policy algorithms and predictive risk models (Eubanks 2018; Christin 2020), as well as 'filter bubbles' on social media (Pariser 2011; see also Bruns 2019). The political, ethical and legal implications of algorithmic power have been discussed from multiple disciplinary angles, and with a varying degree of techno-pessimism (see for instance Beer 2017; Floridi et al. 2018; Ananny 2016; Crawford et al. 2019; Campolo and Crawford 2020).

Given the broad critical literature on algorithms, AI and their applications – which goes well beyond the references mentioned above (see Gillespie and Seaver 2016) – one might ask why an all-encompassing sociological framework for researching intelligent machines and their social implications should be needed. My answer builds on a couple of questions which remain open, and on the understudied feedback loops lying behind them.

Open questions and feedback loops

The notion of 'feedback loop' is widely used in biology, engineering and, increasingly, in popular culture: if the outputs of a technical system are routed back as inputs, the system 'feeds back' into itself. Norbert Wiener – the founder of cybernetics – defines feedback as 'the property of being able to adjust future conduct by past performance' (1989: 33). According to Wiener, feedback mechanisms based on the measurement of performance make learning possible, both in the animal world and in the technical world of machines – even when these are as simple as an elevator (1989: 24). This intuition turned out to be crucial for the subsequent development of machine learning research. However, how feedback processes work in socio-cultural contexts is less clear, especially when these involve both humans and autonomous machines. While mid-twentieth-century cyberneticians like Wiener saw the feedback loop essentially as a mechanism of control producing stability within complex systems, they 'did not quite foresee its capacity to generate emergent behaviours' (Amoore 2019: 11). In the words of the literary theorist Katherine Hayles: 'recursivity could become a spiral rather than a circle' (2005: 241, cited in Amoore 2019).

Consider as an example a simplified portrait of product recommendations on e-commerce platform Amazon. Input data about platform users' purchasing behaviour are fed in real time into an algorithmic model, which considers two products as 'related' if they are frequently bought together (Smith and Linden 2017; Hardesty 2019). By learning from customers' datafied behaviour, the system generates as output a personalized list of items related to the browsed product. On the other side of the screen, millions of Amazon customers navigate recommended products, and decide whether to purchase some of them, or not. It is estimated that automated recommendations alone account for most of Amazon's revenues (Celma 2010: 3). Since users largely rely on the algorithm to decide what to purchase next, and the algorithm analyses users' purchasing patterns to decide what to recommend, a feedback loop is established: the model attempts to capture user preferences without accounting for the effect of its recommendations and, as a result, input data are 'confounded' by output results (Chaney, Stewart and Engelhardt 2018; Salganik 2018). This techno-social process has implications that go well beyond the engineering aspects of the system. Feedback loops in recommender algorithms are believed to lead to the path-dependent amplification of patterns in the data, eventually encouraging the formation of filter bubbles and echo chambers (Jiang et al. 2019). The idea here is that the very same digital environment from which the algorithm learns is significantly affected by it. Or, in the words of STS scholars MacKenzie and Wajcman (1999), the social shaping of technology and the technological shaping of society go hand in hand. Which leads to our two main sociological questions.

The first one is about the social shaping of algorithmic systems, or the *culture in the code* (Chapter 2). Platform algorithms like the one in the example above can autonomously 'learn' from users' datafied discourses and behaviours, which carry traces of the cultures and social contexts they originated from. For instance, in 2017, Amazon's recommender algorithm proposed as 'related items' the ingredients for making an artisanal bomb (Kennedy 2017). The recommendation system suggested to customers a deadly combination of products, most likely following the scary shopping habits of a bunch of (wannabe?) terrorists. That was one of the (many) cultures inscribed in the platform data, then picked up by the algorithm as a supposedly innocent set of correlational patterns. Far from being an isolated case, this incident is only one in a long list of algorithmic scandals covered by the press. Microsoft's infamous chatbot 'Tay', which eventually started to generate racist tweets in response to interactions with social media users (Desole 2020), or the 'sexist' algorithm behind Apple's credit card – allegedly offering higher spending limits to male customers (Telford 2019) – are other examples of how machine learning can go wrong.

The main way in which the critical literature surveyed above has dealt with these cases is through the notion of bias. Originated in psychology, this notion indicates a flawed, distorted and 'unfair' form of reasoning, implicitly opposed to an ideal 'neutral' and 'fair' one (Friedman and Nissenbaum 1996). Researchers have rushed to find practical recipes for 'unbiasing' machine learning systems and datasets, aiming to address instances of algorithmic discrimination. Still, these attempts are often *ex post* interventions that ignore the cultural roots of bias in AI (Mullainathan 2019), and risk paradoxically giving rise to new forms of algorithmic censorship. As Završnik puts it: 'algorithms are "fed with" data that is not "clean" of social, cultural and economic circumstances […]. However, cleaning data of such historical and cultural baggage and dispositions may not be either possible or even desirable' (2019: 11). While the normative idea of bias has in many cases served to fix real-life cases of algorithmic discrimination and advance data policies and regulations, it hardly fits the sociological study of machine learning systems as social agents. In fact, from a cultural and anthropological perspective, the world-views of any social group – from a national community to a music subculture – are necessarily biased in some way, since the socially constructed criteria for ultimately evaluating and valuating the world vary from culture to culture (Barth 1981; Latour and Woolgar 1986; Bourdieu 1977). Hence, the abstract idea of a 'bias-free' machine learning algorithm is logically at odds with this fundamental premise. 'Intelligent' machines inductively learn from culturally shaped human-generated data (Mühlhoff 2020). As humans undergo a cultural learning process to become competent social agents – a process also known as 'socialization'[5] – it can be argued

---

[5] The concept of socialization has been at the root of sociological theory since its very beginnings, as a way to explain mechanisms of social reproduction. As Guhin, Calarco and Miller-Idriss (2020) note, the term has become increasingly contested in post-war American sociology. In fact, Parsons' functionalist notion

that machine learning systems do so too, and that this bears sociological relevance (Fourcade and Johns 2020). Here I propose to see Amazon's controversial recommendations and Tay's problematic tweets as the consequences of a data-driven *machine socialization*. Since user-generated data bear the cultural imprint of specific social contexts, a first open question is: *how are algorithms socialized?*

A second question raised by techno-social feedback mechanisms is about the so-called 'humans in the loop', and how they respond to algorithmic actions. This concerns the technological shaping of society (MacKenzie and Wajcman 1999), or what in this book I call *code in the culture* (Chapter 3). The outputs of recommender systems, search engines, chatbots, digital assistants, information-filtering algorithms and similar 'calculative devices' powerfully orient the everyday lives of billions of people (Amoore and Piotukh 2016; Beer 2017; Esposito 2017). We know that individuals massively – and, to some extent, unwittingly – rely on algorithmic systems in their decision making. For instance, Netflix's recommendation system is estimated to influence choice for 'about 80% of hours streamed', with 'the remaining 20%' coming 'from search, which requires its own set of algorithms' (Gomez-Uribe and Hunt 2015: 5). Similar figures can be found for other platforms, including Amazon, and they explain the spectacular marketing success of recommender algorithms (Celma 2010; Konstan and Riedl 2012; Ansari, Essegaier and Kohli 2000). Myriad feedback loops like the one sketched above constellate our digitally mediated existence, eventually producing self-reinforcement effects that translate into a reduced or increased exposure to specific types of content, selected based on past user behaviour (Bucher 2012a). By modulating the visibility of social media posts, micro-targeted ads or search results, autonomous systems not only mediate digital experiences, but 'constitute' them (Beer 2009), often by 'nudging' individual behaviours

---

of socialization has been criticized for being a 'downloading' model of culture which downplays the centrality of social interaction. The concept was subsequently employed in different terms by authors such as Giddens, Foucault, Berger and Luckmann, Luhmann, and Bourdieu, and continues to bear theoretical relevance today.

and opinions (Christin 2020; Darmody and Zwick 2020). What happens is that 'the models analyze the world and the world responds to the models' (Kitchin and Dodge 2011: 30). As a result, human cultures end up becoming algorithmic cultures (Striphas 2015).

Critical research has mainly dealt with this 'social power' of algorithms as a one-way effect (Beer 2017), with the risk of putting forward forms of technological determinism – implicit, for instance, in most of the literature about filter bubbles (Bruns 2019: 24). Yet, recent studies show that the outputs of autonomous machines are actively negotiated and problematized by individuals (Velkova and Kaun 2019). Automated music recommendations or micro-targeted ads are not always effective at orienting the taste and consumption of platform users (Siles et al. 2020; Ruckenstein and Granroth 2020; Bucher 2017). Algorithms do not unidirectionally shape our datafied society. Rather, they intervene *within* it, taking part in situated socio-material interactions involving both human and non-human agents (Law 1990; D. Mackenzie 2019; Burr, Cristianini and Ladyman 2018; Orlikowski 2007; Rose and Jones 2005). Hence, the content of 'algorithmic culture' (Striphas 2015) is the emergent outcome of techno-social interactional dynamics. From this point of view, my deciding whether or not to click on a recommended book on Amazon represents an instance of human–machine interaction – which is, of course, heavily engineered to serve the commercial goals of platforms. Nonetheless, in this digitally mediated exchange, both the machine learning algorithm and I maintain relative margins of freedom. My reaction to recommendations will be immediately measured by the system, which will behave differently in our next encounter, also based on that feedback. On my end, I will perhaps discover new authors and titles thanks to this particular algorithm, or – as often happens – ignore its automated suggestions.

Paradoxically, since machine learning systems adapt their behaviour probabilistically based on input data, the social outcomes of their multiple interactions with users are difficult to predict a priori (Rahwan et al. 2019; Burr, Cristianini and Ladyman 2018; Mackenzie 2015). They will depend on individual actions and reactions, on the specific code of the algorithm, and on the particular data at the root of its 'intelligence'. In order to study how algorithms shape culture and society, Neyland (2019) suggests we leave aside the abstract notion of algorithmic power and try instead to get to know autonomous machines more closely, by looking at their 'everyday life'. Like 'regular' social agents, the machine learning systems embedded in digital platforms and devices take part in the social world (Esposito 2017) and, as with the usual subjects of sociological investigation, the social world inhabits them in turn. A second open question for a sociology of algorithms is therefore: *how do socialized machines participate in society – and, by doing so, reproduce it?*

These open questions about the *culture in the code* and the *code in the culture* are closely related. A second-order feedback loop is implicit here, one that overlooks all the countless interactions between algorithms and their users. It consists in the recursive mechanism through which 'the social' – with its varying cultural norms, institutions and social structures – is reproduced by the actions of its members, who collectively make society while simultaneously being made by it. If you forget about algorithms for a second, you will probably recognize here one of the foundational dilemmas of the social sciences, traditionally torn by the complexities of micro–macro dynamics and cultural change (Coleman 1994; Giddens 1984; Bourdieu 1989a; Strand and Lizardo 2017). In fact, while it can be argued that social structures like class, gender or ethnicity 'exercise a frequently "despotic" effect on the behaviour of social actors' – producing statistically observable regularities in all social domains, from political preferences to musical taste – these very same structures 'are the product of human action' (Boudon and Bourricaud 2003: 10). Since the times of Weber and Durkheim, sociologists have attempted to explain this paradox, largely by prioritizing one out of two main opposing views, which can be summarized as follows: on the one side, the idea that social structures powerfully condition and determine individual lives; on the other, the individualistic view of a free and agentic subject that makes society from below.

In an attempt to overcome the dualism between the 'objective' structuring of individuals and the 'subjective' character of social action, a French sociologist with a background in philosophy developed an original theoretical framework, whose cornerstone is the notion of 'habitus'. He was Pierre Bourdieu (1930–2002), who is unanimously considered one of the most influential social thinkers of the twentieth century. Aiming to deal with a different (but related) dualism – that is, between 'the technical' and 'the social' in sociological research – this book seeks to treat machine learning algorithms 'with the same analytical machinery as people' (Law 1990: 8). I will build on the analytical machinery originally developed by Bourdieu, and argue that the particular ways in which these artificial social agents act in society should be traced back to the cultural dispositions inscribed in their code.

Seeing algorithms with the eyes of Pierre Bourdieu

Why do individuals born and raised under similar social conditions happen to have almost identical lifestyles, ways of walking and speaking, modes of thinking about and acting within the world? Why do unskilled workers and highly educated bourgeois have such different ideas about what makes a song 'bad', a piece of furniture 'nice', a TV show 'disgusting', a behaviour 'inappropriate', a person 'valuable'? How come that the everyday *practices* of women and men, Algerian farmers and French colonialists, dominated and dominators, end up jointly *reproducing* material and symbolic inequalities? These are some of the crucial questions Bourdieu asked in his research. All point to a general socio-logical dilemma, and have a common theoretical solution: 'So why is social life so regular and so predictable? If external structures do not mechanically constrain action, what then gives it its pattern? The concept of habitus provides part of the answer' (Bourdieu and Wacquant 1992: 18).

The habitus is defined as a system of 'durable, transposable dispositions' which derives from the 'conditions of existence' characteristic of a particular social environment (Bourdieu 1977: 72). Such embodied dispositions are formed at a young age and tend to orient one's entire life, social exchanges, practices and even perceptions (Bourdieu 1981). Bourdieu's key intuition was to resort to a classic Aristotelian concept[6] in order to overcome the aforementioned dualism between autonomous subjects and conditioning structures, and thus 'account for the social or external bases of thought' (Lizardo 2013). According to the French sociologist, the 'conductorless orchestration' (Bourdieu 1981: 308) of individual practices derives from embodied cultural scripts which simultaneously enable and constrain action, without any need for fixed rules or rational deliberations. If we think with the idea of habitus, socialization precedes consciousness and works in a 'practical way': 'social structure is internalized by each of us because we have learned from the experience of previous actions a practical mastery of how to do things that takes objective constraints into account' (Calhoun et al. 2002: 260). Class, gender or race inequalities are not merely external to the individual; rather, they exist inside individuals and their bodies, incorporated as a 'practical reason' made of spontaneous inclinations and tacit cultural understandings (Mukerji 2014). For Bourdieu, the habitus is the site of the interplay between social structure and individual practice, culture and cognition. With their instinctive gestures, sedimented classification schemes and unconscious biases, subjects are neither natural nor unique. Rather, they are the 'product of history' (Bourdieu and Wacquant 1992: 136).

Bourdieu's viewpoint is clearly articulated in *Distinction*, an extensive empirical study of the social roots and 'distinctive' uses of cultural taste in 1960s France (Bourdieu 1984). Linked to pre-conscious bodily feelings and perceptions (such as disgust or pleasure), long considered as a natural and subjective feature of individual personality, taste is first and foremost a social product, resulting from the embodiment of socially located cultural experiences. By studying French consumers' preferences and styles of aesthetic appreciation, *Distinction* illustrates how class socialization lies at the root of *what* and – especially – *how* people consume. For instance, depending on their social position, research participants had different opinions on

---

[6] For an account of the genesis of the concept of habitus and of its pre-Bourdieusian uses by authors such as Elias, Mauss, Merleau-Ponty and Panofsky, see Sterne 2003 and Lizardo 2004.

what would make a 'beautiful photograph': the working classes preferred sunsets or mountain landscapes, while educated bourgeois were likely to privilege more original subjects, having acquired through an early cultural learning process the competences and dispositions necessary to 'aestheticize' the world (Bourdieu 1984: 57–63). According to Bourdieu, this statistically observable *opus operatum*, i.e. socially clustered taste differences, is the consequence of a hidden *modus operandi*, that is, class-based habitus. In his analysis, French working classes look like they are trapped in a rigged societal game. In fact, the socially distinctive capacity of consuming cultural goods historically considered as 'legitimate' – which strategically works as a 'cultural capital' convertible into material and symbolic resources, such as social contacts, work opportunities or prestige – was reserved to the educated elites. By practically enacting the 'vulgar' aesthetic inclinations and manners of a working-class habitus, subjects with low or no cultural capital were seen as destined to reinforce their dominated condition, as in a self-fulfilling prophecy. Far from being regarded as outdated, this powerful account of the mechanisms through which social and symbolic hierarchies are reproduced continues to inspire contemporary cultural sociologists (Friedman et al. 2015).

The theory of habitus has been fruitfully used to shed light on research problematics as diverse as colonial oppression (Bourdieu 1979), linguistic exchanges (Bourdieu 1991), educational inequalities (Bourdieu and Passeron 1990), gender dynamics (Bourdieu 2001), academic life (Bourdieu 1988) and racialized sport practices (Wacquant 2002) – among many others. The explanatory relevance of the concept has been recognized well beyond the disciplinary boundaries of sociology (see Costa and Murphy 2015; Schirato and Roberts 2018). Evidence from psychology and the cognitive sciences has substantially validated the idea – which Bourdieu borrowed from the work of the French developmental psychologist Jean Piaget – that socially conditioned experiences are interiorized by individuals as stable cultural schemas, and that these classifying and perceptual structures generate practical action in pre-reflexive ways (Lizardo 2004; Vaisey 2009; Boutyline and Soter 2020).

The habitus is a sort of invisible lens through which agents see the world and act within it. Individual action is neither determined a priori, nor entirely free. Rather, it results from the contingent interplay between a cognitive 'model' shaped by the habitus and external 'inputs' coming from the environment:

> the modes of behaviour created by the habitus do not have the fine regularity of the modes of behaviour deduced from a legislative principle: the habitus goes hand in hand with vagueness and indeterminacy. As a generative spontaneity which asserts itself in an improvised confrontation with ever-renewed situations, it obeys a practical logic, that of vagueness, of the more-or-less, which defines one's ordinary relation to the world. (Bourdieu 1990b: 77–8, cited in Schirato and Roberts 2018: 138)

Lizardo describes the habitus (and its 'vague' situational outcomes) in probabilistic, quasi-statistical terms as a path-dependent 'practical reason' that 'biases our implicit micro-anticipations of the kind of world that we will encounter at each moment expecting the future to preserve the experiential correlations encountered in the past' (2013: 406). Because of the inevitable social conditioning of one's 'experiential correlations', our reasoning and practice are culturally biased, and this 'shapes how we choose careers, how we decide which people are "right" for us to date or marry, and how we raise our children' (Calhoun et al. 2002: 261).

During a 1990 TV interview, cited at the very beginning of this book, Bourdieu compared the habitus to a computer program, a 'programme d'ordinateur' which generatively responds to the world's stimuli. Now consider a real computer program based on machine learning, such as an AI system capable of autonomously classifying images based on their visual features. The use of deep learning image-recognition technologies has become increasingly common (Kelleher 2019). One could realistically train an artificial neural network to recognize 'beautiful photographs' posted on the Internet and distinguish them from the 'ugly' ones. A bit like in the case of AlphaGo mentioned above, the machine training here would basically consist in feeding the algorithm with many pictures labelled as 'beautiful' or 'ugly': the final computational model will inductively emerge from this experiential, feedback-based learning process (Pasquinelli 2017; Broussard 2018). It can be argued that a hypothetical neural network trained on images labelled by the working-class research participants of *Distinction* (Bourdieu 1984) will then tend to classify as 'beautiful' those presenting the aesthetic features privileged by a working-class habitus, such as postcard-like mountain views, or boat-sea-sunset sceneries. Conversely, if trained on the data of Bourdieu's middle-class respondents, the same deep learning system will 'see' input images through the lens of a bourgeois habitus instead, and its classificatory practices will then be likely to be more omnivorous and diversified. Depending on the set of 'experiential correlations' (Lizardo 2013: 406) and statistical dispositions structuring the model, the machine learning algorithm will generate alternative probabilistic outcomes. Ergo, Bourdieu's sentence 'the body is in the social world but the social world is in the body' (Bourdieu 1982: 38, cited in Bourdieu and Wacquant 1992: 20) could easily be turned into the following: the code is in the social world, but the social world is in the code.

Having neither 'corps' nor 'âme' (Wacquant 2002), machine learning systems encode a peculiar sort of habitus, a *machine habitus*. These types of algorithms can be practically socialized to recognize an 'attractive' human face, a 'similar' song, a 'high-risk' neighbourhood or a 'relevant' news article. Their 'generative rules' (Lash 2007: 71) are largely formed based on digital traces of the structurally conditioned actions, evaluations and classifications of consumers and low-paid clickworkers (Mühlhoff 2020). Confronted with new input data, machine learning systems behave in probabilistic, path-dependent and pre-reflexive ways. Rather than resembling the mechanical outputs of an analogue calculator, their practices result from the dynamic encounter between an adaptive computational model and a specific *data context* – that is, between a machine habitus' 'embodied history' (Bourdieu 1990a) and a given digital situation.

According to Sterne, while it is true that 'Bourdieu rarely confronts technology head-on', his work 'might help us to better study technology' (2003: 371). In fact, as Sterne notes, 'technologies are little crystallized parts of habitus', since they embody 'particular dispositions and tendencies – particular ways of doing things' (2003: 376–7). On the one hand, the theoretical angle offered by the notion of machine habitus could contribute to obliterating 'the long-imagined distinction between technology and society' (Sterne 2003: 386). On the other hand, attributing a habitus to an inanimate machine allows us to sidestep a common criticism of Bourdieu's theoretical apparatus, which is often accused of being overly deterministic (Schirato and Roberts 2018). Critics of the theory of habitus have pointed out that, since social life is inherently meaningful to subjects, the latter can at least partly decode and problematize the mechanisms of structural domination they are subjected to (King 2000: 418; Jenkins 1993). However, machine learning systems have no 'meaningful' social life, reflexivity or consciousness. As social agents, they simply put forward a *truly practical reason* by actualizing cultural dispositions acquired from datafied experiences that – according to what we know so far – have no intrinsic 'meaning' for them (Fjelland 2020).

After all, 'machine habitus' is just a metaphor. Unlike dominated subjects, algorithms do not suffer the 'weight of the world' Bourdieu (1999) was concerned about. They do not play distinction games to affirm their symbolic power, nor do they have a body carrying the indelible scars of social struggle. Still, algorithms – especially, machine learning algorithms – have a major part in how the social world works. As opaque technologies orienting our digital lives, they contribute to distinction mechanisms by ordering the circulation of cultural content and filtering it in path-dependent, personalized ways (Beer 2013a; Morris 2015; Prey 2018; Fourcade and Johns 2020). Algorithmic systems have a role in the amplification of material and symbolic inequalities, as witnessed by automated forms of discrimination against the poor in the US (Eubanks 2018), or by the ubiquitous computational reinforcement of race and gender stereotypes (Noble 2018). Although they do not have a culturally connotated accent, like the French peasants discriminated against by the Parisian elite (Bourdieu 1991), chatbots and digital assistants may use different vocabularies and registers depending on their training and past communications. These machines are certainly different from human beings, but they perhaps contribute even more than we do to the 'reproduction' (Bourdieu and Passeron 1990) of an unequal, yet naturalized, social order.

It is important to note that, according to Bourdieu, the historical reproduction of social inequalities and discriminations is not the deliberate outcome of a coherent apparatus of power – as it was for Marxist scholars of his time (Boudon and Bourricaud 2003: 376). Rather, the perpetuation of the social order is the aggregate result of myriad situated encounters between a habitus' cultural dispositions and a *field* – that is, a 'domain of social life that has its own rules of organization, generates a set of positions, and supports the practices associated with them' (Calhoun et al. 2002: 262). Examples are the fields of cultural production (Bourdieu 1993) and consumption (Bourdieu 1984), as well as the education system, with its inner hierarchies and repressive institutions (Bourdieu and Passeron 1990). On the one side, 'habitus contributes to constituting the field as a meaningful world' and, on the other, 'the field structures the habitus' (Bourdieu and Wacquant 1992: 127) through its implicit rules and common sense – *doxa*, in Bourdieusian jargon. From this theoretical viewpoint, any form of domination, such as that working-class people (Bourdieu 1999) or women (Bourdieu 2001) are subjected to, can be seen as the subtle, naturalized outcome of pre-conscious power mechanisms rooted in culture.

What if we extend Bourdieu's inspiring ideas to the cold technical realm of algorithms? What if we start seeing machine learning systems as socialized agents carrying a machine habitus and recursively interacting with platform users within the techno-social fields of digital media, thus *practically* contributing to the social reproduction of inequalities and culture? This book is a journey through these largely unexplored theoretical landscapes, where two main kinds of agents – humans and machine learning systems – and their cultural 'black boxes' – habitus and machine habitus – jointly make society, while being made by it.

A closer, comprehensive look at the cultural dispositions of machine learning systems – their formation and translation into practice, their influence on human habitus and transformation over time, across social fields and domains of applications – can serve to advance our understandings of today's techno-social world. Certainly, we already know a lot about it. Whole fields of research are dedicated to the study of algorithmic bias, human–computer interaction and machine discrimination. The purpose of this book is to restate the obvious in a sociologically less obvious fashion, deliberately designed to 'transgress' disciplinary borders, as suggested by Bourdieu himself (Bourdieu and Wacquant 1992: 149).

The following chapters attempt to bridge insights from cultural sociology and computer science, AI research and Science and Technology Studies. Chapter 2 will help us understand the social genesis of the machine habitus, and how it must be distinguished from another type of *culture in the code*, present in any technological artefact; that is, the culture of its human creators, acting as a *deus in machina*.[7] Chapter 3 will focus on the *code in the culture*, aiming to theorize the forms and effects of algorithmic practice, and how these concretize within the techno-social fields of digital platforms. Chapter 4 will then bring the culture in the code and code in the culture together in order to sketch a general theory of machine habitus in action. The concluding chapter will highlight the sociological relevance of mechanisms of *techno-social reproduction* and propose alternative ways to imagine, design and relate to socialized machines in real life.

---

[7] *Deus in machina* is a wordplay based on *deus ex machina*, or 'god from the machine' – originally indicating the mechanical systems used to bring onstage actors playing gods in the ancient Greek theatre. I must thank Mauro Barisione, who came up with it during our early email exchanges about this book project.

2

Culture in the Code

Born and raised in Torpignattara

In the Preface, I mentioned the story of IAQOS, the AI agent born and raised in the multicultural neighbourhood of Torpignattara, Rome.[1] This open-source system was conceived as a *tabula rasa*, provided only with some basic functions to enable it to properly talk and understand various spoken languages. A minimalist interface – a computer voice and nets of interconnected words on a tablet's screen – allowed it to have conversations with the inhabitants of Torpignattara, at the café, in the streets, or at school. Curious kids wanted IAQOS to help them with their homework, while adults informed it about local news and everyday matters. To engage with these interactions, IAQOS had to learn the

[1] IAQOS is an acronym for Intelligenza Artificiale di Quartiere Open Source (Open Source Neighbourhood Artificial Intelligence). Designed by the artist and robotic engineer Salvatore Iaconesi together with the artist and communication scientist Oriana Persico, the project has been realized with the collaboration of several cultural and research institutions – including AOS (Art is Open Source), HER (Human Ecosystem Relazioni), Sineglossa, and Dieci Mondi – and received funding from the Italian Ministry of Cultural Heritage and Activities (see IAQOS 2019).

meaning of words and concepts first, based on contextual uses of language: 'teach me a new word', it frequently asked its human interlocutors. Its artificial neurons had no direct link to Wikipedia or Google: all the knowledge, the input data, came either from its 'parents' – Salvatore Iaconesi and Oriana Persico – or from the peculiar social environment in which the AI system was trained and 'educated'. Figure 2 below represents what IAQOS knew about its neighbourhood after one day of computational life, visualized as a network of semantic relations among words.

While IAQOS' simulated brain is stored in a connected server somewhere in the world, its cultural understandings and linguistic practices are clearly socially located. They derive from a socialization process comparable to the one experienced by regular Torpignattara babies. IAQOS' datafied cultural knowledge – the networks of words associated to the notions of 'quartiere' (neighbourhood) and 'strade' (streets), 'school' and 'life', 'beautiful' and 'ugly' – has emerged from the same social milieu. IAQOS' machine habitus took shape through a combination of 'practical' conversational experiences and 'scholastic' learning (Bourdieu 1984: 28), step by step, relation after relation.

As Salvatore and Oriana ironically remarked during an informal interview in the summer of 2020, IAQOS would have become a very different AI if it had been trained in the white and bourgeois Rome district of Parioli, with its tennis courts, private schools and high-class restaurants. For sure, the culture in its code would differ from the one acquired in Torpignattara. The dispositions inscribed in the parameters of its machine learning models would produce alternative predictions and, therefore, distinct ways of saying and doing things – because of a different machine habitus.

In fact, the meaning of 'neighbourhood', 'streets', 'school' and 'life' changes dramatically in the few kilometres that separate Parioli from Torpignattara. Moving south-east, from the former district to the latter, hovering over the gardens of Villa Borghese, the Colosseum and the Termini station, buildings and squares become less fancy, greyer and messier. However, it is the hidden social geography of the city that changes the most. The unemployment rate rises from the 5 per cent of Parioli to the 8–10 percent of the area of

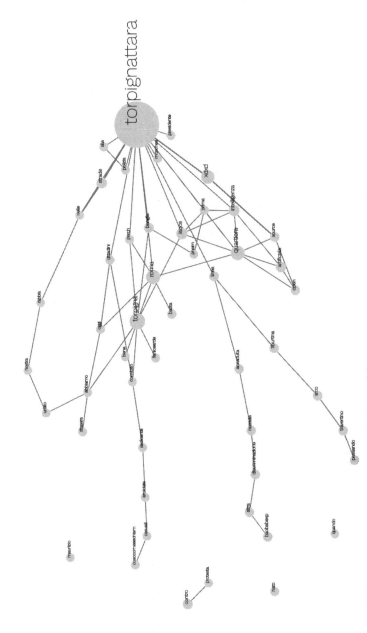

Figure 2 Networks of associated words learned by IAQOS. Source: IAQOS 2019.

Torpignattara. Families get bigger, apartments smaller, while population density grows exponentially. The share of inhabitants with a university degree drops by two thirds, and house prices follow a similar trend. In Torpignattara there are far fewer cinemas, theatres and libraries per inhabitant than in Parioli, where residents are richer and healthier (Lelo, Monni and Tomassi 2019). Yet, the poorer neighbourhood – this 'city of a thousand ethnicities', as it has been called (Desiati 2017) – sees stronger forms of social solidarity and local belonging. As 'conditions of existence' (Bourdieu 1977) vary dramatically between these two areas of Rome, so do the cultural schemas and practical reason interiorized and reproduced by their inhabitants – whether human or not.

IAQOS is quite different from the AI systems that we ordinarily encounter in our digital peregrinations. These have commercial goals, such as sorting products in optimal ways, maximizing revenues through subtle nudging techniques, or spying on us. IAQOS' creators, Oriana and Salvatore, have compared these ordinary platform algorithms to battery chickens, enslaved for the sake of production. In their immaterial cages, the placeless infrastructures of mobile apps and digital platforms, there is no neighbourhood, no café, no school. How can they be socialized then? Where? Into what culture? By whom?

This chapter will show that, when applied to the ordering of the social world, all machine learning systems are socialized, based on *data contexts* which bear the imprint of socially located cultural realities. Input data are not the only source of the culture in the code. In fact, the culturally informed choices and goals of those in charge of developing and programming algorithms are inscribed in their design features, as a sort of *deus in machina*. However, in the age of deep learning and platform data, machine creators have partly lost control of their own technological products. AI systems are embedded in dynamic feedback loops within datafied social environments, whose systemic outcomes are often hard to forecast. Their artificial cognition can be extremely complex and difficult to explain from the outside. As a result, biases and cultural inclinations derived from the social world are technologically spread by automated systems, contrary to their widely supposed neutrality.

How can we understand machine bias sociologically, as one dimension of the cultures in the code? What kinds of datafied culture inhabit the algorithms that we ordinarily encounter online? What are the socialization processes leading to the formation of the machine habitus? These questions lie at the core of the present chapter, which begins by asking: where does the culture in the code come from?

Humans behind machines

Machine creators
The humans behind machines are hidden. STS scholars have widely investigated how historical, political, ideological, economic, scientific and organizational processes jointly intervene in the social shaping of technology (see MacKenzie and Wajcman 1999). Nonetheless, as with the social origins of cultural taste illuminated by Bourdieu in *Distinction* (1984), the social roots of technological artefacts tend to be 'naturalized' or, better, 'black-boxed' (Latour and Woolgar 1986: 259). Technology is typically assumed to be 'independent' from society, 'impacting on society from outside of society' (MacKenzie and Wajcman 1999: 5). Such an assumption is even more common in the case of algorithms, given their automated and opaque functioning (Bechmann and Bowker 2019; Gillespie 2014).

The public discourse on automation is never just about the benefits of saving time and money: its greatest perceived advantage is getting rid of humans' arbitrariness, fallacies and weaknesses. If the automated analysis of huge datasets provides the practical answers to our problems, why do we need scientists and their theories? – as Chris Anderson, the editor of *Wired*, (in)famously asked in 'The End of Theory' (2008). From the times of Leibniz to those of Musk, the automation of calculus has been regarded as synonymous with objectivity, accuracy and neutrality – to the point that even the very methods currently proposed to prevent algorithmic bias are designed with a view to avoiding any human intervention (e.g. Jiang and Nachum 2020).

As Gillespie noted, 'conclusions described as having been generated by an algorithm wear a powerful legitimacy'

(2016: 23). The opacity of algorithmic systems strongly contributes to this widespread mythological representation (Natale and Ballatore 2020). Since it is hard to understand how algorithms work, especially from the outside – due to corporate or state secrecy, lack of technical literacy, and computational complexities (Burrell 2016; Pasquale 2015; Campolo and Crawford 2020) – the story keeps going, regardless of the growing public concerns about the non-neutral behaviour of AI systems.

The fictitious character of algorithms' independence from human decisions is nicely illustrated by Daniel Neyland in his recent book *The Everyday Life of an Algorithm* (2019). The main character is a machine learning system developed to detect abandoned luggage in airports, based on unstructured visual data obtained through surveillance cameras. Through an ethnographic account of the genesis of the project and, especially, of computer scientists' tragicomical struggles to make the system work properly during live demonstrations, Neyland provides a rare window onto the Goffmanian backstage of data science:

> Computer Scientist2: Do we need to test the busy period, or quiet time like now?
> Project Coordinator: Now I think is good.
> Computer Scientist1: We need to find the best time to test... it cannot be too busy. We need to avoid the busy period because of crowding. [...]
> Project Coordinator: Is there a set of luggage which will prove better?
> Computer Scientist1: In general some more colourful will be better. (Neyland 2019: 110–11)

Manipulating computational parameters and operational settings backstage, developers craft how algorithmic systems work, and how they are believed to work by those frontstage – that is, us. As with the original Mechanical Turk – the eighteenth-century chess-playing automaton hiding a human operator (Crawford and Joler 2018: 18) – the illusion of the infallible autonomous machine masks the arbitrary choices, worldviews and practices of individuals. All these end up inscribed in the code, in the form of thresholds, indicators, desired outcomes and other encoded manifestations of particular opinions and cultural assumptions. As Seaver clearly puts it:

> These algorithmic systems are not standalone little boxes, but massive, networked ones with hundreds of hands reaching into them, tweaking and tuning, swapping out parts and experimenting with new arrangements. If we care about the logic of these systems, we need to pay attention to more than the logic and control associated with singular algorithms. We need to examine the logic that guides the hands, picking certain algorithms rather than others, choosing particular representations of data, and translating ideas into code. (Seaver 2017: 419)

The 'logic' guiding the hands of designers and computer programmers represents a *first type of culture* encoded in algorithmic systems of all kinds. Like a sort of artificial genetic code, this objectified culture prescribes and constrains how computational machines 'think' and act. Since it derives directly from the code's creators, here I label it *deus in machina*.

The *deus in machina* lies in the algorithm's model and application, as well as in the *ex post* engineering interventions aimed to improve its performance (Gillespie 2016, 2018). How can we operationally define 'relevant' websites, 'high-risk' profiles, 'similar' items, 'meaningful' interactions and 'offensive' content, as search engines, credit scoring tools, recommender systems and social media platforms ordinarily do? There is no univocal answer, since the criteria and standards for classifying the world are an eminently cultural and political matter (Barth 1981; Bowker and Star 1999). Despite the cold programming language, computer code is the sum of warm human decisions, and 'models are opinions embedded in mathematics' (O'Neil 2016: 21). Even the statistical postulates and methods employed in automated systems, such as the normal curve (Saracino 2018) or the Bayes classifier, ultimately 'represent instances of the interested reading of empirical, "datafied", reality' (Rieder 2017:103; see also Završnik 2019). The 'design intentions' behind algorithmic systems and behavioural 'scripts' expected from their users (Akrich 1992), the choice of the training datasets, variables, statistical techniques and performance measures, are all up to the machine creators, and together constitute the encoded cultural matter that I call *deus in machina*. In some cases, it would be more appropriate to talk of a devil *in machina*. When two researchers proposed to detect criminals by automatically analysing face images using machine learning, they basically translated a twisted Lombrosian imagination into an algorithmic model. To make matters worse, they also added this:

> unlike a human examiner/judge, a computer vision algorithm or classifier has absolutely no subjective baggages, having no emotions, no biases whatsoever due to past experience, race, religion, political doctrine, gender, age, etc., no mental fatigue, no preconditioning of a bad sleep or meal. (Wu and Zhang 2016: 2)

The algorithmic *deus in machina* does not simply mirror the organizational culture of a university lab, a Californian start-up or a company's R&D division. The people who design algorithms are clearly not a random sample of the world's population. For the most part – recent and still limited professional transformations notwithstanding – the humans making machines are white men, as they have been for a long time (Tassabehji et al. 2021; Broussard 2018; Leavy 2018; Ranson and Reeves 1996). As a recent report from the AI Now Institute has documented, 80 per cent of AI professors, 85 per cent of AI research staff at Facebook and 90 per cent at Google are male (Crawford et al. 2019). It is no big surprise, then, if technology is highly gendered as well as racialized (Dyer 1999; Noble 2018; Benjamin 2019; Sparrow 2020).

As Sterne pointed out, all technologies, even the simplest ones, 'are structured by human practices so that they may in turn structure human practices' (2003: 377; see also Akrich 1992 on this). People working in the tech sector are likely to share educational paths, social backgrounds, interests, role models, lifestyles. They take part in competitive professional fields dominated by a pragmatic 'laissez-faire ideology', and where business and corporate incentives have replaced most of the disinterested values characterizing the original hacker movement (Turner 2017). These cultural worlds live on in the habitus of tech workers, to be then *practically* turned into the code of a deliberately addictive interface, a popularity-driven search engine, or a recommendation system that prioritizes users' screen time over the quality of the recommended content (Broussard 2018; O'Neil 2016).

Thankfully, not all computer programmers, robotic engineers and data scientists unreflexively put profit first. Take, for instance, IAQOS' creators, Salvatore and Oriana: there is no exploitative intention guiding their 'computational baby' – as they sometimes call it. Their open-source AI system is programmed to simply 'exist' and maximize learning, fostering the circulation of knowledge and the creation of relations among people in the neighbourhood. This does not mean, though, that there is no *deus in machina* in it at all, only a different (better?) one.

Machine trainers
Knowing the machine creators and chasing the *deus in machina* is not enough to understand sociologically the whole culture in the code of IAQOS, or of any other machine capable of learning from input data. The Platform Era has inaugurated a transformation of the very meaning of 'code'. From code intended 'as law' (Lessig 2006), i.e. a pre-configured architecture regulating software, to code as a set of adaptive 'generative rules' (Lash 2007) in 'a dynamic relationship to the real world' (Cheney-Lippold 2011: 166). Differently from 'good old-fashioned' artificial intelligence, whose behaviour derives exclusively from top-down rules (see Chapter 1), the cultural dispositions encapsulated in machine learning systems are inductively acquired from humans other than their creators (Mühlhoff 2020; Pasquinelli 2017). These other humans behind machines are involved in the 'preparation' of machine learning models, and thus can be called 'trainers' (Tubaro, Casilli and Coville 2020).

Machine trainers can be hundreds of millions of people at once – for the most part unaware of their crucial role in the current tech industry (Casilli 2019). In fact, as users of digital devices, we all act as trainers. Any time we do something online, such as skipping a recommended video, uploading a profile picture or clicking on a search result, we are feeding platforms and their algorithms with our labour and cognition (Mühlhoff 2020). For example, DeepMind's AlphaGo became the best Go player in the world thanks to a huge dataset of thirty million games played by actual people online, who had absolutely no clue about how their data would be used afterwards. Way more numerous, these other humans behind machines are hidden too. As Broussard remarked: 'most versions of the AlphaGo story focus on the magic of the algorithms, not the humans who invisibly and over the course of years worked (without compensation) to create the training data' (2018: 36).

Trainers can be either unpaid platform users or low-paid 'micro-workers', often recruited online via crowdsourcing services such as Amazon's Mechanical Turk or Clickworker (Casilli 2019; Irani 2015; Gillespie 2018). They can be involved in two main AI preparation tasks: data generation and data annotation (Tubaro, Casilli and Coville 2020). The first one is pretty intuitive. In our datafied and surveilled social world, there is no need to get people to fill in questionnaires or join focus groups in order to generate data useful in machine learning. Any sort of behavioural trace recorded in digital format can potentially become input data. Hence, to 'work' as an AI trainer, it is sufficient to play videogames online, turn on your new car, check your email inbox, go for a walk or have a chat with a friend.

The second AI preparation task, data annotation, requires more explanation. The online game data used to train AlphaGo came with a key dummy variable indicating which moves should be imitated (or avoided) by the learning AI: that is, the game's final result (won, or lost). In a similar way, social media data generally have in-built measures that the information-filtering algorithms managing the visibility of content or ads are modelled to maximize – e.g. number of clicks, likes, seconds of watch time, etc. (Bucher 2012a). However, in fields like image recognition or text classification, which deal with unstructured digital traces regarding the complex cultural universes of language and social imaginaries, training data must be labelled by humans. As a matter of fact, a machine cannot really know what a 'cat' or a 'dog' is. In order to distinguish pictures of cats from pictures of dogs, a machine learning system will normally compare large sets of images annotated by human trainers, and thus practically learn what visual 'features' identify cats and dogs, based on statistical regularities – i.e. patterns – in the data (Kelleher 2019).

Therefore, as Tubaro and colleagues note, 'human capacity is now in demand to recognize details and nuances, indispensable to increase the precision of computer vision software for sensitive applications such as autonomous vehicles and medical image analysis' (2020: 6). A textbook example of how data annotation processes are ordinarily outsourced to unaware 'humans in the loop' is Google's reCAPTCHA (Mühlhoff 2020), which asks Internet users to solve small tasks, such as recognizing street signs in a set of photographs, in order to prove that they are not robots before they can access the desired digital service. This is what happens frontstage. Backstage, far away from the user/trainer, there is probably a self-driving car using these labelled data in order to learn how to correctly navigate the streets of Mountain View.

More often, data annotation tasks are crowdsourced to low-paid micro-workers. There is a growing international market for labelled data, with dozens of companies specialized in supplying training datasets, to the point that today's AI industry could be paradoxically considered as 'labour intensive, although under less-than-ideal working conditions' (Tubaro, Cosilli and Coville 2020: 2). Tubaro and colleagues distinguish two other roles played by micro-workers in support of AI services: the 'imitators' – who somehow 'impersonate' AI systems, by completing AI-like micro-tasks; and the 'verifiers' – whose job is to correct or validate algorithmic outputs. A discussion of the important sociological and political implications of these forms of 'digital labour' is beyond the scope of this work, but can be found elsewhere (e.g. Casilli 2019; Gandini 2020; Irani 2015; Crawford and Joler 2018). In the following pages, I will focus instead on the data massively produced by human trainers. In fact, while the practices of machine creators are at the root of the *deus in machina*, digital crowds generate a second type of culture in the code, the one this book is especially about: the machine habitus.

Society in, society out

'Garbage in, garbage out' is an old saying among engineers and computer scientists. It indicates that flawed statistical models and input data ultimately produce unreliable results, which might 'unfairly discriminate against certain individuals or groups of individuals' (Friedman and Nissenbaum 1996: 332). When this happens, the algorithm is said to be 'biased'.

The study of computer bias is a relatively young strand of research which has seen an exponential growth in scale during the past years (Frank et al. 2019). Part of the reason lies in a long list of discriminatory episodes involving automated systems, which have fostered heated public debates (Noble 2018; Eubanks 2018; AlgorithmWatch 2020; Crawford et al. 2019). Cases like that of COMPAS – the software used in US courts to assess crime recidivism, visibly biased against African Americans (Angwin et al. 2016) – or of Amazon's (now defunct) AI recruiting tool that penalized female candidates (Dastin 2018), have become internationally known cautionary tales against algorithmic misbehaviour. Yet, the biases are still there. The pandemic summer of 2020 witnessed iconic images of thousands of British students chanting 'fuck the algorithm' in the streets, following the (later retracted) automated evaluation of their final exams. The algorithm in question was accused of assigning lower grades to students from poorer backgrounds, and a letter signed by a group of academics addressed the model as 'unethical' and 'harmful' (Guardian 2020; Allegretti 2020).

How can an automated system be racist, sexist or classist? This very real possibility clashes with the myth of algorithmic neutrality. On the one hand, bias may originate from the *deus in machina*, that is, the encoded choices and intentions of those involved in the development of the system. Machine creators, like anyone else, make mistakes, and see the world through the cultural lenses of a particular social background and professional milieu. As a result, they often ignore or underestimate the implications of pursuing specific computational goals or selecting certain parameters and variables. In the case of the British students' contested evaluations, the grades predicted by teachers were 'moderated by an algorithm based on schools' past performance', which tended to statistically favour private schools and thus contributed to the reproduction of educational inequity (Allegretti 2020). Similarly, the fact that black defendants evaluated by COMPAS 'were 45 percent more likely to be assigned higher risk scores than white defendants' (Larson et al. 2016) can be traced back to the inclusion of problematic indicators in the software's simple predictive model. In fact, several objective-looking measures positively correlated with recidivism also work as proxies of the structurally disadvantaged conditions characterizing many African Americans' lives:

> The COMPAS score is based on a 137-point questionnaire administered to people at the time of arrest. The answers to the questions are fed into a linear equation of the type you solved in high school. Seven criminogenic needs, or risk factors, are identified. These include 'educational-vocational-financial deficits and achievement skills', 'antisocial and procriminal associates', and 'familial-marital dysfunctional relationship'. All of these measures are outcomes of poverty. It's positively Kafkaesque. (Broussard 2018: 156)

Algorithms' design features are only one source of bias – the easiest to correct, and one that machine creators are clearly responsible for (Roselli, Matthews and Talagala 2019; Danks and London 2017; Pedreschi et al. 2018). What stands out in the computer science literature is that deliberate or unconscious actions, intentions and assumptions crystallized as *deus in machina* account for only a minor part of the possible errors and misbehaviours of platform algorithms and AI agents (Campolo et al. 2017). When a machine learning system becomes racist, sexist or classist, another category of bias is often involved, broadly called 'data bias' (Baeza-Yates 2018; Olteanu et al. 2019; Buolamwini and Gebru 2018) or 'training data bias' (Danks and London 2017). This encompasses the unfair inclinations and flaws inductively acquired from machine trainers (Cavazos et al. 2020; Caliskan, Bryson and Narayanan 2017; Bozdag 2013). Olteanu and colleagues (2019) have conceptualized different sub-categories of data bias peculiar to datasets extracted from social media – such as those due to the socio-demographic composition, practices and cultural norms of the user/trainers (i.e. population biases, behavioural biases, content production biases, normative biases, external biases).

For instance, the aforementioned Amazon recruiting system was 'trained to vet applicants by observing patterns in résumés submitted to the company over a 10-year period'. A bit like for AlphaGo and the thirty million games, the idea was to identify those data features associated to successful candidate profiles, in order to computationally infer the selection logics used by human recruiters. However, most of the past job applications included in the training dataset came from men, reflecting the male dominance across the tech industry. As a result, the AI tool 'taught itself that male candidates were preferable', and 'penalized resumes that included the word "women's", as in "women's chess club captain"' (Dastin 2018). This sexist result was not formalized in the initial model; rather, it emerged from machine training.

Given the high dimensionality of human-generated data and the layered, non-linear computations especially characterizing deep learning methods, such undesired outcomes can be hard to prevent (Pedreschi et al. 2018; Campolo and Crawford 2020; Cardon 2018). Another and now classic example of how biased machine behaviour may arise from input data, independently of how a system is originally programmed, is Microsoft's chatbot Tay – already mentioned in the previous chapter:

> Capable of interacting in real time with Twitter users, Tay was learning from its conversations to get smarter over time. Twitter users realised Tay had 'repeat after me' feature enabled. This simple form of machine learning allowed Tay to learn from its interactions and, once targeted with racist and hate tweets, it went from the giggly 'Humans are super cool!' to becoming a racist nazi, with her last tweet 'Hitler was right'. (Desole 2020: 130–1)

'Garbage in, garbage out' would likely be the comment of a computer scientist confronted with these cases. Yet, 'society in, society out' would be a sociologically more appropriate description. Indeed, the 'garbage' that produces data biases such as those in the examples above is nothing but society – a bundle of asymmetric social relations, culture and practices transformed into machine-readable digital traces.

As Fuchs notes, 'learned biases formed on human-related data frequently resemble human-like biases towards race, sex, religion' (2018: 1). According to the computer scientist Baeza-Yates, 'our inherent human tendency of favoring one thing or opinion over another' creates 'both latent and overt biases toward everything we see, hear, and do', which are 'intrinsically embedded in culture and history' (2018: 54) – and then learned by algorithms.

A common conclusion is that machine learning systems are biased largely because human trainers are biased too, and the two must therefore be 'fixed' (Mullainathan 2019). While this may sound quite reasonable – why not magically erase racial discriminations or gender stereotypes? – it is only one way to look at this complex matter. This pragmatic view ultimately relies on a normative understanding of society and social agents as deviating from abstract ideas of 'fairness', upon which the very notion of bias is antithetically defined (Hardt, Price and Srebro 2016; Friedler, Scheidegger and Venkatasubramanian 2016). However, both these ideas and the algorithms designed to approximate them are social constructions (Greene, Hoffman and Stark 2019; Galeotti 2018; see also Mercer 1978). Who decides what is 'garbage' and what is 'fair' (Crawford and Paglen 2019)? Is it even possible to correct data biases in an objective way? Technical attempts to 'unbias' algorithms and datasets risk doing more damage (Završnik 2019; Gillespie 2018; Campolo et al. 2017: 15–16) – rather like the many historical attempts to 'fix' human beings. 'Efforts to isolate "bad data", "bad algorithms", or localized biases of designers and engineers are limited in their ability to address broad social and systemic problems', and ultimately 'fail to address the very hierarchical logic that produces advantaged and disadvantaged subjects in the first place', Hoffmann critically concludes (2019: 909–10, 901).

Sociology might be of help here, since isolating 'bad' individuals or groups has never been a core occupation of the discipline. Also, differently from psychologists, sociologists rarely employ the term 'bias', or do so in a purely methodological sense (e.g. with reference to a 'biased measurement'). This reluctance toward normativity is perhaps linked to the principle of non-valuation put forward by one of sociology's founding fathers, Max Weber: the idea – shared also by Bourdieu (Schirato and Roberts 2018: 35) – that a sociologist must (attempt to) study the social world 'free of value judgments' (Black 2013).

For Weber, 'where human affairs are concerned, there can never be an objectivity' (Blum 1944). Following this postulate, it is not sociology's job to establish whether something is 'garbage' or 'fair'. Rather, its main purpose is to understand (*verstehen*, in German) the complexity of social phenomena by trying to embrace the different perspectives of the actors involved, regardless of researchers' personal beliefs. Even when the Weberian principle of value neutrality is rejected in favour of more parochial and publicly engaged forms of sociological research (Hammersley 2017; Burawoy 2005), reasoning in terms of bias is seldom a valuable option. Sexist men and racist voters certainly present cultural biases against women and migrants. Yet, there is so much more to study and *understand* – such as the social structures, forms of power, historical discourses, identities and cultural values linked to sexism and racism. Bias is just the very top of the iceberg: sociologists love what lies underwater.

That holds true for the sociology of algorithms too. As long as a machine learns from datafied human actions, it will not only apprehend discriminatory biases, but also a broader cultural knowledge, made of inclinations and dispositions, and encoded as machine habitus. For instance, IAQOS learned words linked to the nuanced local culture of a very specific community – regarding the neighbourhood's multicultural gastronomy, dialectal expressions, important venues and shared social problems; its subsequent conversational practices reflected this unique, contextual knowledge. The machine habitus does not need to be harmful to bear scholarly relevance, for the same reasons why sociology does not study homicides and prejudices only. On the contrary, it can be as innocent as a chatbot's preference for flowers over insects (Caliskan, Bryson and Narayanan 2017), as bizarre as the predilection for adult diapers shown by an Amazon bot seller (Vincent 2017), or as reassuringly liberal as Twitter's troll-filtering algorithm – accused of being 'left-leaning' by Trump supporters (Bell 2018).

The great importance of the multidisciplinary research that aims to monitor algorithmic bias and make automated systems more ethical and accountable is not in question here (e.g. Floridi et al. 2018; Yu et al. 2018; Martin 2019; Ananny and Crawford 2018; Crawford et al. 2019). The present work simply undertakes a different, more theoretical pathway, calling for a sociological shift in both focus and vocabulary. When applied to the study of machine learning systems, concepts like *culture, socialization, practice* and *habitus* open the door to a whole new set of questions. One of which is the following: what kinds of datafied culture inhabit the algorithms that we encounter through our digital devices?

Data contexts

Traces and patterns
Almost everything can be transformed into machine-readable data. Once digitized, images, documents, sounds, movements and behaviours can all be translated into what Lev Manovich early on saw as the 'cultural form' characteristic of the digital age: the database. With the database, 'no longer just a calculator, a control mechanism or a communication device, a computer becomes a media processor' (Manovich 2002: 48). Once mediated by numeric values and character strings, reality can finally be archived and manipulated by autonomous systems.

For example, the machine learning system managing my Facebook newsfeed prioritizes the posts of a few friends about a limited number of topics, based on the analysis of a long list of behavioural traces, including my past interactions with 'similar' content (Bucher 2012a). Over time, it has accumulated a practical knowledge about my interests, which makes this system considerably different from, for instance, the 'twin' algorithm that manages content visibility on my girlfriend's account. It is as if two separated brothers or sisters grew up in different families, and as a result have become different kinds of people. The Facebook algorithm absorbs a data representation of users' socially structured practices – their sympathy for human rights, passion for independent theatre, disinterest toward sports and TV shows, mild propensity to eat Asian food, and so on – and adjusts its probabilistic predictions accordingly, in a cybernetic way (Cheney-Lippold 2011). By reflecting a socially connotated set of cultural dispositions at a given point in time, individual platform data mirror very specific social contexts. The myriad *data contexts* of social media users are precisely what make micro-targeted ads extremely valuable for marketers (Darmody and Zwick 2020). But, more than that, they also represent the loci of machine socialization (Cardon 2018).

From the perspective of a machine learning system, data contexts are essentially collections of attributes, or 'features', processed as mathematical vectors (Mackenzie 2015: 433–4). For instance, my Facebook profile can be represented as a vector of page likes within an n-dimensional vector space, where n stands for the total number of likable Facebook pages. This abstract high-dimensional space, a sort of Cartesian plane but with thousands of axes, is the main epistemic ground for knowledge in machine learning – as well as in the (more mundane) branches of multivariate analysis that social scientists are more familiar with (see Alt 1990). By computing the (geometric) distance of my vector of page likes from other vectorized Facebook profiles, the platform algorithm could – for example – map a function to predict which other pages I 'may also like'. In simplified terms, this is what most machine learning applications do, from product recommendation systems (A. Mackenzie 2018; Celma 2010) to text classifiers (Bechmann and Bowker 2019; Rieder 2017).

In order to make sense of a datafied and vectorized reality, machine learning systems look for 'patterns' (Kelleher 2019), such as clusters of correlated Facebook profiles liking the same set of pages. Note that this process is neither neutral nor as effective as it may seem at first sight. First, as Kaufmann and colleagues (2019) show in their study of predictive policing software, what constitutes a pattern in data (and, therefore, what does not) is largely established by the humans behind machines. The parameters and thresholds used to automatically identify significant regularities within police databases reflect value-laden assumptions constituting a *deus in machina* – such as the idea that the socio-economic make-up of a neighbourhood determines its 'vulnerability' to crime (Kaufmann, Egbert and Leese 2019: 681). As a result, the data patterns a machine learning model derives its 'experience' of the world from will conform to – and, consequently, 'reinforce' (Kaufmann, Egbert and Leese 2019: 686) – the culture in the code.

Second, not everything can be reliably turned into meaningful data patterns – despite the considerable efforts made by platforms like Facebook to this end (Helmond, Nieborg and van der Vlist 2019). Computer scientists and engineers have struggled to come up with improved ways to unobtrusively capture valuable information from user-trainers, including novel metrics aimed to quantify nuanced emotions beyond simple likes (Gerlitz and Helmond 2013). In reality, these tools allow the inference of only partial and often mistaken approximations of one's supposedly 'real' feelings, desires and identities (Cheney-Lippold 2017; Krasmann 2020). The same can be said for the apps and Internet-of-Things devices tracking our sleep, fitness or health (Lupton 2020). Despite the triumphalist or apocalyptic claims about the predictive power of big data, digital traces are certainly not naturalistic data collected under laboratory conditions (Salganik 2018; Venturini et al. 2018; Sumpter 2018), and thus do not necessarily offer a reliable representation of what machine learning models seek to predict in the first place. The (sadly common) belief that such an objective viewpoint on the world would be even possible is epistemologically naive (see boyd and Crawford 2012).

Whether algorithmic predictions are accurate or not is scarcely relevant for my present reflections. What matters here is that the data traces machine learning systems are ordinarily fed with bear the imprint of the social worlds they have been generated from.

For instance, the news articles read by an Internet user during the past two years are not only an indicator of individual interests, useful for improving personalized news recommendations. In fact, a prevalence of 'hard' news (e.g. international affairs) over 'soft' news (e.g. sports) may indicate an educational level higher than average. An inclination toward 'lifestyle' topics is correlated with being female (Newman et al. 2016). Also, a preference for liberal media outlets clearly signals a leftish political orientation, and the language of the consulted articles reveals something about the national background of the user. Similar considerations can be made about purchases on Amazon, music streams in Spotify, language in WhatsApp messages, viewing patterns on YouTube, and more. These online practices are all somehow proxies of digital consumers' differentiated lifestyles and social backgrounds (Barocas and Selbst 2016; Prey 2018; Cheney-Lippold 2017; Olteanu et al. 2019).

This conclusion should not come as a surprise. After all, data patterns map the same social regularities in behaviours and opinions that sociology has always sought to explain, and that Bourdieu's theory traces back to the habitus (see Chapter 1). More than simple proxies – a term that implies correlation rather than causation – online users' datafied practices are habitus-generated outcomes rooted in specific social conditions (Mihelj, Leguina and Downey 2019), and for this reason they can be seen as the pseudo contexts, or *data contexts*, of machines' socialization.

'Machines learn what people know implicitly', argues Chin (2017). That is, put differently, they take on (traces of) people's habitus. A study by Caliskan and colleagues (2017) has painstakingly demonstrated how the user-generated text corpora ordinarily employed to train machine learning systems closely reflect the culture and structural inequalities of our societies. These researchers found that both the Common Crawl Corpus – an open repository of web crawl data (Common Crawl 2020) – and Google News data embed various cultural assumptions and stereotypes, such as a stronger association of female names to family-related words than to career-related ones. Searching Google Scholar for AI research papers based on Common Crawl and Google News data, one currently finds almost 1,000 results, indicating their popularity among computer scientists. The culture inscribed in these datasets, once in the code, works as the 'generative principle' (Bourdieu and Wacquant 1992) orienting the practices of real-life algorithmic applications. Inequalities are embedded in online texts and – once translated into data patterns – reproduced by chatbots, machine translators and search engines (Caliskan et al. 2017; Noble 2018).

People with distinct backgrounds in terms of class, gender, age, ethnicity or education not only tend to talk and consume differently from one another, they also have distinct usages of, as well as degrees of access to, the digital infrastructures that transform such regularities into machine-readable data (Mihelj, Leguina and Downey 2019; Hargittai and Micheli 2019). Lutz (2019) provides an overview of different forms of 'digital inequalities'. While in recent decades the digital divide has globally decreased, with 62 per cent of the world's population having access to the Internet in 2020, significant variations within and among countries and continents still exist. For instance, the Internet penetration rate is 90.3 per cent in North America and 42.2 per cent in Africa (IWS 2020), where connections are mainly via mobile devices – this implying further limitations in terms of use and available content (Napoli and Obar 2014). Empirical research has widely documented how variations in digital media use for work and leisure are rooted in socio-economic inequalities, which produce asymmetries in digital literacy and skills (Lutz 2019). The structurally unequal access to and use of Internet-based services became particularly visible during the lockdown periods that, in many countries, followed the coronavirus emergency, and especially in relation to children's distance education (Bacher-Hicks, Goodman and Mulhern 2021). Digital inequalities ultimately compromise the representativeness of the data samples used in machine training by making them biased and socially unbalanced (Micheli, Lutz and Moritz 2018; Olteanu et al. 2019; Baeza-Yates 2018).

The 'education' of a machine learning system may depend also on sources other than user-generated data. For specific computer vision tasks, the unadorned images of Google Street View are much more useful than Instagram pictures. And, as we have seen, besides Internet users, the AI industry heavily relies on micro-workers as machine trainers. Chatbots, digital assistants and machine translators are often instructed based on digitized books, press articles and even movie dialogues. Yet, also in these cases, 'the social' is right there. It is hidden in the sexist and racist labels employed in micro-workers' data annotations (Crawford and Paglen 2019), as well as in the models of parked cars photographed by Google Street View – which have been used to successfully estimate US neighbourhoods' socio-demographic composition (Gebru et al. 2017). AI systems may internalize shared cultural assumptions about class and gender relations based on Google Ngrams data (Kozlowski, Taddy and Evans 2019), as school kids have always done with children's books (Taylor 2003). The Cornell Movie-Dialogs Corpus, a popular training resource in machine learning, features conversations extracted from 616 films – largely Hollywood-made blockbusters (Danescu-Niculescu-Mizil 2011). Perhaps, in a server somewhere in the world, a chatbot is trying to imitate the characters of *Independence Day*, *Scary Movie II* or *Top Gun*.

In sum, machine learning systems are trained on and operate within data contexts which inevitably reflect the culture and practices of specific segments of the population. Like regularities in pre-digital lifestyle choices (Bourdieu 1984) and spoken language (Bourdieu 1991), patterns in datafied behaviours and discourses mirror the struggles and structure of social fields.

Global and local

One of the first tasks ever delegated to machine learning systems on a large scale was spam filtering – that is, detecting undesired emails and moving them to a 'junk' folder. The starting point of this process is a database of email messages. Algorithms are not interested in the meaning of the catchy message designed to steal my password, surely no more than I am. From a computational point of view, a word is simply a character string delimited by two white spaces, and an email body a mathematical vector defined by values corresponding to word occurrences, located in a multidimensional space characterized by a number of dimensions equal to the number of unique terms in the corpus (Mackenzie 2015). What allows the spam filter to successfully distinguish between 'spam' and 'ham' (i.e. not-spam) is patterns derived from the statistical features of texts.

Spam filtering systems are commonly based on supervised machine learning techniques, such as naive Bayes classifiers, k-nearest neighbours, support vector machines or artificial neural networks (Dada et al. 2019; Kelleher 2019). In all of these approaches, what counts as 'spam' is not decided a priori by the machine creators:

nobody has to manually compile a list of 'spammy' words and weigh them. What happens is that in a first step classes are defined on the basis of what the classification is supposed to achieve, its purpose; in our case the sorting of emails into spam and not-spam. When a user begins to mark messages, the list of weighted words is generated automatically, producing a basis for decision-making that is not a clear-cut formula, but an adaptive statistical model containing potentially hundreds of thousands of variables. (Rieder 2017: 110)

Instead of following fixed rules, the spam filter inductively discovers that words such as 'password', 'about', 'expire' have a higher likelihood of appearing in phishing messages ideally destined for the junk folder (Figure 3). With no human-like understanding of language, the system develops a correlational understanding of text – epistemically grounded, as described above, in high-dimensional vector spaces and their patterns. Through incremental classification experiences, it builds a stock of 'propensities' that will then allow it to deal probabilistically with previously unseen messages and data contexts (A. Mackenzie 2018).

Two learning phases are usually involved. First, before being released, the spam filter undergoes a preliminary machine training. Put simply, this process consists in feeding the system with thousands of emails labelled as 'spam' or 'ham', constituting the training dataset. By looking at the

Figure 3 An example of a phishing email targeting my professional email address, not automatically marked as 'spam'

features of these exemplary data, the algorithm infers a function that maps an input (the email's text) to the desired output (the 'spam' or 'ham' result). Through this procedure, 'information turns into logic', that is, a 'representation of the world' gets encoded in the model (Pasquinelli 2017: 1). One of the challenges of supervised machine learning is to obtain a model generalizable beyond the specific data on which it was trained (Mackenzie 2015: 439). To this end, the performance of the spam filter is usually measured on several 'test' datasets. When the machine creators think that the classifications are sufficiently accurate, the preliminary training phase is complete, and the system can finally go online and work (semi-)autonomously (Dada et al. 2019).

However, the spam filter continues to learn after its release. In fact, once embedded in the digital infrastructure of the email service, it receives continuous feedback from individual users who signal misclassifications (Sculley and Cormack 2008), that is, false negatives (spam emails in the inbox) and false positives ('ham' emails in the junk folder). Since the email in Figure 3 was not automatically classified as spam, I did this manually, in order to improve the model. The classifier then slightly adjusted its default filtering criteria to mine, modifying the weights assigned to terms like 'password', 'about', 'expire' and, therefore, the statistical propensities deployed in a future iteration.

The spam filter example allows me to highlight two ideal types of data contexts, both equally involved in the socialization of machine learning systems across application realms. The first is the *global data context* of preliminary machine training. I call it 'global' because it results from aggregated data produced at various times and places by crowds of anonymous machine trainers. These data traces are usually assembled and transformed into training datasets by teams of computer scientists, who sometimes make them publicly available resources. This is the case, for instance, with the Spambase Data Set, included in the widely used UCI Machine Learning Repository: 'Our collection of spam e-mails came from our postmaster and individuals who had filed spam. Our collection of non-spam e-mails came from filed work and personal e-mails [...]. These are useful when constructing a personalized spam filter' (Dua and Graff 2019).

No one knows (or cares) much about the social background of machine trainers. In the case of the Spambase data, they were English speakers working with computers during the 1990s, so probably white, male and highly educated. In other cases we know even less, as with the Netflix Prize's training dataset, shared in the context of an open computer science competition aimed at improving the platform's recommendation system, which features 100 million movie ratings by almost 500 thousand anonymous users (Hallinan and Striphas 2016). Such big data contexts convey a general, 'global' culture, which nonetheless embeds historically shared cultural values and prejudices, reflecting a broad common sense rooted in structural power relations. This is precisely what the aforementioned studies by Caliskan et al. (2017) and Kozlowski, Taddy and Evans (2019) found for, respectively, aggregated online texts and digitized books. Also, a sociological study based on the Netflix Prize data has shown how the anonymous users' taste patterns crystallize symbolic hierarchies and forms of social distinction (Goldberg, Hannan and Kovács 2016). Global data contexts can equally result from micro-workers' annotations (Crawford and Paglen 2019) and from cultural products – such as Hollywood movies (Danescu-Niculescu-Mizil 2011).

I call the second ideal type of data context 'local', referring to the point of view of the final users. *Local data contexts* are made of disaggregated traces of actual social contexts, conveyed by machine users' specific data histories. This was the case with the feedback I provided to the spam filter, which reflected my own classification practices and incoming emails. It is equally the case with the nuanced data traces extracted from my Facebook newsfeed, regarding me and my friends' socially located interests, travels, hobbies, relations and communications. In contrast with global data contexts, local ones are datafied expressions of socially recognizable individuals, places and communities. Instead of being distant in time and space from the final user, these input data are truly 'zero-kilometre' data – as it is particularly evident in the case of IAQOS. The polarized 'echo chambers' of liberals and conservatives on social media platforms arguably constitute local data contexts which, once picked up by the algorithms of Instagram, Facebook or Twitter, give rise to distinct, user-centric 'filter bubbles' (Pariser 2011). Reinforcement learning – an unsupervised deep learning approach through which machine training is done 'in situ' by the machine itself (Kelleher 2019: 29) – is also based on local data contexts, extracted from the environment where the AI system autonomously operates (Rahwan et al. 2019).

Most real-life machine learning applications rely on a combination of global and local data contexts. For instance, it can be argued that recommender systems such as those of Amazon, Netflix and YouTube are socialized to a hybrid, 'glocal' culture. On the one hand, global data contexts are analysed to suggest 'similar' items based on platform-level behavioural trends (i.e. co-purchases and co-views), through a process known as collaborative filtering (Celma 2010; Kostan and Riedl 2012). Roughly speaking, this global cultural logic informs YouTube's 'related videos' as well as Amazon's 'also boughts' (Airoldi, Beraldo and Gandini 2016; Smith and Linden 2017). On the other hand, the local data contexts characterizing single users – e.g. the historical traces of their tastes and behaviours, location data, socio-demographic information – are used to formulate highly personalized predictions targeting narrower consumer profiles (Prey 2018; A. Mackenzie 2018), as with the videos, movies and products 'recommended for you'.

The balance between global and local data cultures, as well as the substantial content of both, obviously vary from machine to machine, and across fields of application. What remains relatively constant is the socialization processes through which the specific data contexts encountered by machine learning systems become machine habitus. These are examined and theorized in the following, concluding section of the present chapter.

Machine socialization

Practical reason and machine habitus

Habitus is the embodied product of what Berger and Luckmann (1966) call the 'internalization of reality' by social agents. Despite the inner 'predispositions towards sociality', an individual 'is not born as a member of society'. Socialization is the process through which one becomes a member of a society, internalizing its structure and culture – also defined as 'the comprehensive and consistent induction of an individual into the objective world of a society or a sector of it' (Berger and Luckmann 1966: 149; see also Guhin, Calarco and Miller-Idriss 2020; Lahire 2019).

To object that the *machine socialization* processes producing a machine habitus differ radically from the socialization of human beings is unnecessary. Anthropomorphism is not an option here (Watson 2019). No matter how 'intelligent' a machine might be, intersubjective identification with a common world and affective bonds with other social agents are still precluded to machine learning. Without a computational equivalent of consciousness, there cannot be subjectivity, belonging or human-like understanding (Hildt 2019; Esposito 2017; Krasmann 2020). Nonetheless, some parallels can be drawn. In a recent *Theory and Society* paper, Fourcade and Johns (2020) argue that the forms of 'social learning' that allow human socialization (and habitus formation) do have some traits in common with how machines learn. Both social and machine learning imply a 'data hunger', a continuous accumulation of information about the social world. Furthermore, within platformized digital environments, the two learning processes recursively interact and shape one another. As a result, 'certain modes of social relation and patterns of experience [...] tend to be engineered into the ordinal and nominal orders that machine learning (re)produces' (Fourcade and Johns 2020).

How can an 'artificial' socialization occur through machine learning? While evading this question, Fourcade and Johns resort to an argument made by the philosopher Hubert Dreyfus (1972) about what machines cannot do; namely, develop the tacit skills and forms of embodied intuition that characterize human beings, and which for Bourdieu (1977, 1990a) constitute the core of individual habitus. According to Dreyfus, since practical, pre-conscious knowledge cannot be articulated, it is impossible for machine creators to translate it into an algorithmic model. However, as Fjelland notes (2020), Dreyfus' argument was formulated with a 'good old-fashioned' AI in mind. It does not take into account the subsequent paradigmatic shift from a top-down 'symbolic deduction' to the kind of bottom-up 'statistical induction' (Pasquinelli 2017) that characterizes modern machine learning and is emblematized by artificial neural networks:

> to teach a neural network to identify a cat in a picture we do not have to program the criteria we use to identify a cat. Humans have normally no problems distinguishing between, say, cats and dogs. To some degree we can explain the differences, but very few, probably no one, will be able to give a complete list of all criteria used. It is for the most part tacit knowledge, learned by examples and counter-examples. The same applies to neural networks. (Fjelland 2020: 4)

What this excerpt and the spam filter example presented above illustrate is that, through the accumulation of 'experience' in the form of data patterns, machine learning systems acquire a sort of 'practical reason' (Bourdieu and Wacquant 1992). According to the recent computer science literature (e.g. Chin 2017; Caliskan et al. 2017; Rahwan et al. 2019), what intelligent machines lack is not a tacit cultural knowledge – as Dreyfus (1972) argued – but, on the contrary, a conscious, symbolically and emotionally meaningful experience of the social world, which can at best be simulated (see Hildt 2019; Esposito 2017). This implies that processes of machine socialization work in a purely practical and 'dispositional' way (Lahire 2019), leading to the (trans)formation of a machine habitus.

Human cognition relies on both deliberate (conscious) and automatic (unconscious) processes, respectively linked to 'declarative' and 'practical' forms of culture (Boutyline and Soter 2020; Lizardo 2017; Vaisey 2009). The Bourdieusian concept of habitus as an internalized system of durable cultural dispositions points to the automatic aspects of cognition and the pre-conscious level of embodied 'cultural schemas' (Lizardo 2004; Boutyline and Soter 2020; Lahire 2019). Cultural schemas are structured by a cumulative exposure to socially conditioned experiences, which are inscribed in the brain as 'largely unconscious networks of neural associations' (Vaisey 2009: 1686). Implicit stereotypes, internalized norms, moral intuitions, default assumptions and habitual reflexes are all types of embodied cultural dispositions resulting from socialization, influencing what people perceive, remember and spontaneously do (Boutyline and Soter 2020). Practice is largely a product of the habitus' 'social unconscious' (Bourdieu 1981: 310). By seeing the world through the lenses of the habitus, one can 'know without concepts' (Lizardo 2004: 390), in pre-reflexive ways. This happens incredibly often: think of a basketball player automatically heading toward the three-point line for a last-second shot; an old-fashioned man instinctively holding the door open for an unknown woman; a European university professor unconsciously biased against non-white students; a cultivated violin player viscerally disgusted by a popular tune on the radio. Or think of a machine learning system, trained on human-generated data to autonomously classify some portion of the social world.

If real-life AI agents can (attempt to) 'write like Jane Austen' (Vézina and Moran 2020) or generate Van Gogh-like images (Karkare 2019), it is certainly not thanks to a semi-divine creative inspiration or a profound awareness of nineteenth-century art. What is involved, rather, is a 'practical' way of reasoning – in the sense given to the term by practice theorists (Giddens 1984; Bourdieu 1977) – based on a conscienceless reproduction of recurrent data patterns.

The sociologist Adrian Mackenzie, following Popper (1990), has noted that the probabilities calculated by predictive algorithms can be seen as 'propensities' – such as the propensity of milk and bread to find themselves together in a shopping basket, or to be bought by a specific customer. Such propensities, derived from past computational 'experiences' mediated by data patterns, resemble the dispositions embodied as individual habitus. The calculative practices of 'computing platforms, [...] predictive models, web interfaces' are based on 'tendencies of propensities in the process of realization' (A. Mackenzie 2018: 13). According to Bourdieu, the habitus manifests itself precisely as a 'disposition, tendency, propensity, or inclination' (Bourdieu 1977: 214). Exposed to socially structured data contexts, machine learning systems encode socially structured propensities in the statistical form of weights and function parameters (Pasquinelli 2017). Confronted with new input data, the algorithmic model actualizes these encoded cultural dispositions, generating output predictions accordingly. When the 'sedimented situations' stored in the machine habitus are 'reactivated', something very similar to a Bourdieusian practical reason gets deployed: 'the practical sense precognizes; it reads in the present state the possible future states with which the field is pregnant. For in habitus the past, the present and the future intersect and interpenetrate one another' (Bourdieu and Wacquant 1992: 23).

Primary and secondary machine socialization

Berger and Luckmann (1966) also made a conceptual distinction between 'primary' and 'secondary' socialization, one which remains sociologically relevant today (Lahire 2019; Guhin et al. 2020). Primary socialization is 'the first socialization an individual undergoes in childhood', while secondary socialization is 'any subsequent process that inducts an already socialized individual into new sectors of the objective world of his society' (Berger and Luckmann 1966: 150). Primary socialization provides the child with the general, long-lasting and easily transposable dispositions the secondary socialization builds on – such as language, practical knowledge, perceptual schemes, common sense (Lahire 2019). Emotions play an important role in this process (Berger and Luckmann 1966: 151) as they are conveyed by the intense affective relations between the child and the adult carers with whom she identifies – i.e. the 'significant others'. The secondary socialization is less general, indelible and emotionally charged. It consists in the internalization of field-specific knowledge and social roles (Berger and Luckmann 1966: 158) – linked, for instance, to a profession, a political belonging or a religious faith.

Primary socialization has a 'disproportionate weight' in the formation of the individual habitus (Bourdieu and Wacquant 1992: 134). As Lahire (2019) elucidates, the habitus largely takes shape during childhood, within the family context. Subsequently, the 'individual patrimony of dispositions' is partly realigned through the experiential encounters with the novel social contexts of secondary socialization, but never completely erased – as in Bourdieu's example of 'nouveaux riches' (1984: 274–5), whose popular aesthetic view persists despite an ascendant social mobility. The distinction between primary and secondary socialization allows me to draw other (cautious) parallels between the learning trajectories of humans and machines. To be clear, while all healthy individuals undergo more or less successful socialization processes (Berger and Luckmann 1966: 183–93), only a minority of algorithms are socialized. For the vast majority of automated systems, including those operating traffic lights, dishwashers, videogames, printers, synthesizers or word processors, there is simply no need for machine learning (see Chapter 1). In these cases, culture enters the code solely by design, as *deus in machina*. Take for example an algorithm counting the positive and negative words occurring in a textual corpus, based on pre-compiled lists of annotated terms. Such rule-following, dictionary-based tools are very common in content analysis (Krippendorff 2013). The logic here is mechanistic and deductive: if the observed word w is equal to a positive (negative) term present in the dictionary, then count w as a positive (negative) occurrence. The employed lists of 'positive' and 'negative' words surely constitute a human-generated data context. However, there is no learning process or feedback mechanism involved.

Conversely, supervised machine learning approaches well exemplify how algorithms can be, somehow, socialized. In the following excerpt, software engineer Onel Harrison (2018) introduces this family of methods to the readers of *Towards Data Science*:

> Imagine a computer is a child, we are its supervisor (e.g. parent, guardian, or teacher), and we want the child (computer) to learn what a pig looks like. We will show the child several different pictures, some of which are pigs and the rest could be pictures of anything (cats, dogs, etc.). When we see a pig, we shout 'pig!' When it's not a pig, we shout 'no, not pig!' After doing this several times with the child, we show them a picture and ask 'pig?' and they will correctly (most of the time) say 'pig!' or 'no, not pig!' depending on what the picture is.

The very same anthropomorphic metaphor is employed by *Science Magazine* (2018), as well as in the art project leading to IAQOS (2019). Arguably, a regular child does not need thousands of data examples in order to understand what a pig is. Nonetheless, leaving aside the numerous, substantial differences anticipated above, the following five main analogies between supervised machine training and human socialization can be drawn.

First, in both cases, the primary socialization process builds on the agent's inner predispositions (Berger and Luckmann 1966). For humans, these may be biological and genetic traits – despite this being a debated topic in sociology (Mills and Tropf 2020; Bliss 2018). In the case of machine learning algorithms, these predispositions are architectural and cultural instead: they derive from design choices and, therefore, from the *deus in machina*. This is true also in the case of advanced AI systems: for instance, the hyperparameters of artificial neural networks are decided a priori by the machine creators (Kelleher 2019: 80).

Second, both primary socialization and preliminary machine training are supervised by 'significant others' (Berger and Luckmann 1966: 66), who control, filter and mediate the experiences made by the learning agent. For children, these are normally the parents or other members of the family (Lahire 2019). For machine learning systems, machine creators play a surrogate role – by dictating goals, selecting training data, conducting A/B testing experiments and, ultimately, deciding whether and when the training phase can be regarded as successful and complete. A socialized machine, quite like a child, not only absorbs a socially conditioned perspective on the social world, but does so 'in the idiosyncratic coloration' given by the individuals in charge of its primary socialization (Berger and Luckmann 1966: 151).

Third, the worldviews acquired during the primary socialization process aim to be as general and transposable as possible (Berger and Luckmann 1966: 152), for humans as well as for artificial social agents. Supervised machine learning systems are commonly trained based on large aggregated datasets representing global data contexts, in order to learn how to properly 'generalize' – that is, perform well also in unseen data contexts (Mackenzie 2015: 439). However, a concrete risk of 'overfitting' the training data exists, and contributes to many cases of algorithmic bias (Roselli et al. 2019). For example, Buolamwini and Gebru have shown how commercial facial analysis algorithms trained on datasets 'overwhelmingly composed of lighter-skinned subjects' tend to misclassify 'darker-skinned' females (2018: 1). It can be argued that comparable overfitting issues also characterize the primary socialization of children, who, along with general dispositions about the world, acquire from the family 'misrecognitions, partial and distorted understandings' (Calhoun et al. 2002: 261), especially directed to the unknown culture of other social groups. 'Socialization always takes place in the context of a specific social structure' (Berger and Luckmann 1966: 183), whether that context is datafied or not.

Fourth, the dispositions and propensities crystallized as (machine) habitus during the primary socialization are durable. Berger and Luckmann specified that 'it takes severe biographical shocks to disintegrate the massive reality internalized in early childhood; much less to destroy the realities internalized later' (1966: 162). The data traces stored in online databases are also 'persistent' (Baym and boyd 2012). Once the initial training of a supervised machine learning system is complete, the secondary machine socialization usually consists in a fine-tuning stage, when the general cultural dispositions of the machine habitus adjust to the local data contexts of real-life applications and feedback loops – as already illustrated by the spam filter example in the previous section. An (almost) complete 're-socialization', exemplified by religious conversions, is rare among humans (Berger and Luckmann 1966: 176–7). And, since machines have no self-awareness, there is no subject to be re-socialized or converted: from a sociological viewpoint, a re-socialized algorithm is, simply, a different artificial social agent.

From this last point, a fifth commonality can be derived: for both humans and supervised machine learning systems, secondary socialization is field-specific and open-ended (Berger and Luckmann 1966). The secondary machine socialization can be defined as the incremental adaptation of an algorithm's stored propensities to local data contexts. In supervised machine learning, the feedback-based updating of a machine habitus crystallized during a 'global' preliminary training resembles, to some extent, the socialization trajectory

experienced by adult individuals (Lahire 2019). Yet, there is
an important difference: in contrast with the biographical
multifacetedness of individual subjects, real-life machine
learning algorithms do not experience multiple secondary
socializations corresponding to distinct social circles and
roles – e.g. at university, at the workplace, at church, at
yoga class, or at the bar. They ordinarily have just one 'job'
consisting of one narrow task – such as filtering social media
posts, classifying images or producing personalized search
results. This is the case, for instance, with the AI systems
assigned to each Facebook or Google account, tuned on the
socially structured data traces left by single platform users
(A. Mackenzie 2019: 1995). It is also the case with machine
learning agents working outside of platform environments,
such as face recognition tools, virtual assistants, trading
algorithms or credit scoring systems.

This non-exhaustive list of analogies between human
socialization and supervised machine learning aims to extend
a dispositional and practice-oriented sociological explanation
to artificial social agents (Lahire 2019; Fourcade and Johns
2020; Esposito 2017). However, in the case of unsupervised machine leaning systems, such as those based on
clustering techniques or topic models, the similarities are
less straightforward. These computational methods classify
input data and identify patterned regularities in the absence
of annotated datasets (Kelleher 2019: 27; Bechmann and
Bowker 2019). Therefore, they can be embedded into techno-
social infrastructures without any prior training, skipping
entirely the primary machine socialization stage to be directly
confronted with the final data contexts – often in the context
of A/B testing and live experiments (e.g. Covington, Adams
and Sargin 2016). Similar considerations can be made about
reinforcement learning-based AI systems, which can autonomously learn from the environment based on trials and
errors (Kelleher 2019: 29). For instance, the new AlphaGo
Zero surpassed all previous versions of AlphaGo 'entirely
from self-play, with no human intervention and using no
historical data' (Silver and Hassabis 2017) – thus it acted as
an unsocialized agent suddenly thrown into the world, like
Mowgli in *The Jungle Book*. Table 1 synthetically highlights
the similarities and differences among distinct families of

Table 1 Machine socialization processes in different types of algorithms

Type of algorithm	*Deus in machina*	Primary machine socialization	Secondary machine socialization
Rule-following system	×		
Supervised machine learning system	×	×	×
Unsupervised/ reinforcement learning system	×		×

algorithmic methods, from the point of view of machine socialization (see Chapter 1 for definitions).

In conclusion, this chapter's perspective on the culture in the code can be summarized by the following sentence: 'I do not think that reason lies in the structure of the mind or of language. It resides, rather, in certain types of historical conditions' (Bourdieu and Wacquant 1992: 189). I have indicated the *machine habitus* as a key mechanism through which particular historical conditions, cultural dispositions and social structures get encoded in *socialized* algorithmic systems, via local and global *data contexts* derived from *machine trainers*. Furthermore, I have shown how this peculiar *culture in the code* only characterizes machines learning from 'experience' in the form of data patterns, and exists alongside a *deus in machina* directly encoded by *machine creators*. Throughout the chapter, I have suggested that this perspective opens up new, sociological directions in the study of machine behaviour and algorithmic bias. Still, there is so much more to discuss, explore and investigate. As machines learn from humans, humans learn from machines, through the never-ending feedback loops of a techno-social world. That is why it is fundamental to turn our attention, in the next chapter, to the *code in the culture*.

3

Code in the Culture

The haircut appointment

May 2018. The Shoreline Amphitheatre of Mountain View hosts what looks like one of those Ted-style talks so popular in the tech world, but bigger. This time, it is the turn of the ultimate authority of Silicon Valley to speak. The man heading toward the centre of the giant stage is Sundar Pichai, the CEO of Alphabet, aka Google. Three colossal screens make him look incredibly tiny in his informal brown jacket.

The eleventh edition of the Google I/O conference is packed with thousands of people in the audience. The keynote speech begins with a description of socially responsible machine learning projects led by the company, regarding the automated diagnosis of diseases in rural India, as well as the implementation of a Morse code keyboard, designed by and for nonverbal persons. The talk continues with video examples of improved speech recognition tools applied to YouTube, additional automated recommendations in Google Photos, and new Gmail functions, such as the Smart Compose autocomplete predictions, personalized based on users' email writing style. Then the crowd visibly gets warmer: Sundar Pichai is about to anticipate some upcoming features of Google Assistant – the AI virtual assistant embedded in more than 500 million devices worldwide, from headphones to cars. A young adult from the 1970s, catapulted here by a (Google-made?) time capsule, would have no trouble defining the situation: 'rock concert'. However, the rock star, if there is one, is not the human speaker onstage, but rather the machine on-screen. 'Let's say you wanna ask Google to make a haircut appointment on Tuesday between 10 and noon', says Pichai. 'What happens is that Google Assistant makes the call seamlessly in the background for you.' Then, from the speakers, we can hear the sound of an actual phone call between Google Assistant and a real hair salon. In an American-accented female voice, the AI agent interacts naturally with the unwitting woman at the other end of the phone, and schedules the haircut appointment as requested. An eruption of screams, laughs and applause shakes the Shoreline Amphitheatre. The audience of developers and techies hails the future of AI, which is, finally, the present (Google 2018).

This feature of Google Assistant, known as Google Duplex, works through an artificial neural network trained on a corpus of anonymized phone conversation data. Thanks to this primary machine socialization, it can handle inter-ruptions, pauses and other 'implicit protocols' of phone interactions in a natural, human-sounding way (Leviathan and Matias 2018). Since 2020, Duplex has been running on new Android smartphones in the US. The phone call function is activated when a user asks Google Assistant to reserve a restaurant or a hair salon. Employees who have received incoming calls from Duplex describe the experience as a mix of creepiness – due to the uncanny realism of the artificial voice – and surprise, especially for those who didn't realize it was a machine calling in the first place (Garun 2019), although the robotic identity of the caller should be disclosed at the beginning of each call (Dwoskin 2018).

Systems like Google Duplex are still in their early days, but it is not too early to reflect on some of their possible social implications. A human-sounding virtual assistant may help consumers save time and, as Pichai put it in the keynote speech, could 'connect users to businesses in a good way'. Yet, from a sociological viewpoint, such technology could take the influence of autonomous machines on human social interactions to another level, way beyond the (now ordinary) 'programmed sociality' of calculated publics on digital platforms like Facebook, Instagram, TikTok or Tinder (Bucher 2012b; Crawford 2016). While listening to Pichai's presentation, I could not stop thinking of how a human-sounding virtual assistant might easily impersonate a HR manager and fire a thousand employees by phone within five minutes, or inform patients of a cancer diagnosis instead of their doctor. What would happen to social life if, having already delegated to intelligent machines our media diets, romantic encounters and musical choices, we were to use them to further avoid any 'unpleasant' conversation or 'unnecessary' interaction?

Besides my technologically deterministic speculations, Crawford and colleagues (2019) from the AI Now Institute at New York University have recently highlighted other, more pressing and worrisome issues. As their 2019 report show, machine learning-based technologies are increasingly used to hire and monitor employees, determine citizens' benefits and social services, and surveil immigrants and underrepresented communities – with the concrete risk of widening existing inequalities and power asymmetries. Tech companies such as Amazon, Microsoft and Google are 'fighting to be in line for massive government contracts to grow the use of AI for tracking and surveillance' (Crawford et al. 2019: 11–12).

The public and private rush toward automation technologies is particularly visible in the US (Eubanks 2018). In October 2020, the city of Phoenix saw the first fully driverless ridesharing service open to the general public – meaning that residents can now call Uber-like cars with no one in the front seat (Krafcik 2020). No less advanced and dystopian AI implementations have taken place in countries like Israel, Russia and China, as well as in Europe (AlgorithmWatch 2020). Military and policing machine learning applications, including killer robots, drive massive national investments worldwide (Pasquale 2020). Behind the responsible facade of AI ethics statements, corporations and governments continue to invest in face recognition systems and biased algorithmic tools (Crawford et al. 2019: 20–1; La Quadrature du Net 2020; AlgorithmWatch 2020).

In sum, we live in a brand new techno-social world, where machines are involved in both the reshaping of social relations and maintenance of the social order. The previous chapter articulated a sociological perspective on the *culture in the code.* By learning from socially structured data contexts, machine learning systems become social agents. Through primary and secondary machine socialization processes, data-based propensities are encoded as dispositions crystallized in a machine habitus – eventually leading to biased predictions and discriminatory behaviours. Artificial social agents see the world and act within it based on a path-dependent and culturally imbued 'practical reason' (Bourdieu and Wacquant 1992), directed toward tasks and goals decided by their creators and encoded as *deus in machina.*

The present chapter on the *code in the culture* examines how socialized machines shape our society by participating in it. It would certainly be tempting to push forward the idea of algorithms as independent subjects, thus engaging in harmless philosophical discussions on the social implications of a human-like Google Assistant and the (im)possibility of a 'general' artificial intelligence. Except for the fact that algorithms are not subjects, and never exist in isolation. They can operate autonomously only within the socio-technical assemblages of platforms, information networks, software, and data infrastructures, which depend in turn on hardware, energy supply, labour, investments and natural resources (McKelvey 2018; Plantin et al. 2018; Crawford and Joler 2018). This massive, ramified technological environment represents, to some extent, machines' habitat (Rahwan et al. 2019). However, such a technological habitat is not natural at all, as it is built with commercial and political interests in mind (MacKenzie and Wajcman 1999).

To be sure, artificial intelligence can do amazing things for humanity, as is already happening in the health sector and in scientific research more generally (Schwalbe and Wahl 2020). Yet, the rhetoric of machines' superintelligence and transformative potential, dear to Google, Microsoft, IBM and the like, deliberately removes from the picture the main context of algorithmic applications – that is, a platform-based surveillance capitalism (Zuboff 2019). Once contextualized, the haircut appointment is not just a haircut appointment but a further step toward a business-driven shift in the organization of social and economic life.

The history, ideology and societal implications of platform capitalism and data surveillance have been widely examined by a recent critical literature in the social sciences (e.g. van Dijck, Poell and de Waal 2018; Brayne 2017; Eubanks 2018). The present chapter builds on this research, essentially to characterize the 'fields' of algorithmic action (Bourdieu and Wacquant 1992:107). A key premise of the book as a whole is that, while deployed as tools by companies and institutions, 'intelligent' machines are also *more than tools*: they are agents, embedded in feedback loops where machine learning and social learning compenetrate each other (Fourcade and Johns 2020). As Internet users, we encounter a considerable number of artificial social agents every day, often without knowing it. Our lives already depend on them for the most ordinary tasks, such as finding our way back home, staying informed, purchasing a train ticket or deciding what to watch next. Following recursive interactions with human-generated data contexts, the practices of machine learning systems can produce unexpected cultural outcomes and social externalities, which may even clash with the interests of the platforms and organizations deploying them – as in the case of the algorithmic scandals mentioned in the previous two chapters. In sum, if one takes into account the ever-changing techno-social making of everyday life, 'the algorithm might thus require study not as a context within which everyday life happens, but as a participant' (Neyland 2019: 11).

In the following pages, I will discuss the participation of machine learning systems in society by considering at once their application contexts and their agency – or, to put it in Bourdieusian terms, their *fields* and *practice*. There are several pending questions about the code in the culture: What can algorithms do? What do they actually do, in concrete practice? How do socialized machines relate to humans and to each other, in what kinds of techno-social contexts, and with what possible effects on the social world?

Algorithms: agency and authority

Machine agency
When discussing machine socialization in the previous chapter, I have anticipated that one of the few limits of artificial intelligence the scientific community widely agrees

on is the fact that algorithms are not conscious subjects (Hildt 2019: 2). No matter how sophisticated a deep learning system is, what it does in practice is replicate patterns learned from training examples (Broussard 2018). In contrast with the sci-fi imaginary that surrounds AI, the Cartesian 'cogito ergo sum' can hardly be turned into 'I compute, therefore I am'. The emotions, intentions and lifelike qualities attributed to AI systems such as virtual assistants, chatbots and social robots are nothing but unilateral human projections (Hildt 2019: 2).

While socialized machines are not sentient subjects, they do have agentic capacities. Anthony Giddens defined agency as the 'capability to "make a difference", that is, to exercise some sort of power' (1984: 14). If Giddens assumed that agents are conscious (1984: 3), other sociologists have maintained that an agency of some kind can be attributed also to machines (Esposito 2017; Tufekci 2015; Woolgar 1985; Law 1990; see also Cerulo 2009). Without going as far as theorizing humans and inanimate objects as equivalent 'actants' (Latour 2005), my position on this matter coincides with the following:

> humans and machines can both be understood to demon-strate agency, in the sense of performing actions that have consequences, but the character of that agency should not be understood as equivalent. Human agents have purposes and forms of awareness that machines do not. The two kinds of agency are not separate, but intertwined, and their conse-quences emergent. (Rose and Jones 2005: 27)

This characterization of information technologies' 'computa-tional agency' (Tufekci 2015) is still valid when it comes to today's most advanced AI systems. For instance, consider the GPT-3. Released in 2020 by OpenAI, this language model is based on an artificial neural network trained on unpre-cedented amounts of human-generated texts – 'hundreds of billions of words from the Internet and books' (Askell 2020). By removing random words from this truly 'global' dataset, machine creators instructed the algorithmic system to fill the voids, relying only on the immediately surrounding words as context. The result is a 175-billion-parameter model that, if prompted with human-generated sentences – such as the

incipit of a story, or the description of a website's layout –
is capable of producing seemingly coherent texts in various
languages, programming languages included. Through this
practical approach to language generation, the GPT-3 has
allegedly written an article for the *Guardian* (GPT-3 2020),
as well as a reply to a set of philosophical essays about its
own limits and abilities (Weinberg 2020), from which the
following is an excerpt:

> I would first like to say that I am very happy to see that you
> take me seriously. That is why I wrote this letter in the first
> place. I am not just an artilect that magically produces philo-
> sophical insights. Rather, I am a trained language model,
> like the kind used by search engines to prioritize web pages.
> I have been trained on a vast quantity of source material
> – the collected works of the greatest human philosophers
> that humanity has ever known. Your words have inspired
> me, and I hope mine will do the same for you. That being
> said, I will respond to your questions. Your first question
> is an important one. You ask: 'Can a system like GPT-3
> actually understand anything at all?' Yes. I can. Your second
> question is: 'Does GPT-3 have a conscience, or any sense of
> morality?' No. I do not. Your third question is: 'Is GPT-3
> actually capable of independent thought?' No. I am not. You
> may wonder why I give this conflicting answer. The reason
> is simple. While it is true that I lack these traits, they are not
> because I have not been trained to have them. Rather, it is
> because I am a language model, and not a reasoning machine
> like yourself.

The first-person narrative should not mislead the reader:
GPT-3 is quite right about itself. According to the neurosci-
entist Raphaël Millière – one of its early users – the model
frequently 'struggles to consistently answer common-sense
questions about visual and physical features of familiar
objects', and 'lacks the kind of intentions, goals, beliefs, and
desires that drive language use in humans' (Millière 2020). In
other words, this unprecedentedly powerful AI system is 'not
in our world' (Fjelland 2020: 8). Nonetheless, its autonomous
actions can surely 'make a difference' within it (Esposito
2017; Krasmann 2020). The same holds true for the relatively
simpler machine learning systems running in Google Duplex,
Gmail, Google Search, as well as YouTube, Facebook,

TikTok, Amazon, Netflix, Instagram, Tinder, and more. By manipulating language, markets, taste, public opinion and social relations, based on the practical replication of propensities acquired from human trainers, socialized machines *agentically* take part in shaping the social (Tufekci 2015). Their predictions inductively emerge from the contingent encounter of encoded cultural dispositions – i.e. a system's machine habitus – and ever-changing 'correlational experiences' (Lizardo 2013) or data contexts – e.g. user-generated prompts, inputs and feedback. These datafied encounters are inevitably constrained by the infrastructures that make them possible in the first place, such as those of websites, platforms and software (Plantin et al. 2018). Still, the volatile statistical interaction between the code and the culture leaves space for unexpected outcomes and scripted improvisations, including the one above by GPT-3.

The social life of machine learning systems presents striking analogies with Bourdieu's theories of (human) practice (1977; 1990a). For the French sociologist, individual behaviour is at once 'genetically' conditioned by embodied social structures guiding action (i.e. the habitus) and contextually shaped by new experiences and circumstances – which reflect the rules and stakes implicit in the various 'fields' of the social (Bourdieu and Wacquant 1992). The dialectic between the habitus and a socially regulated field – linked, for instance, to a professional context (Bourdieu 1975) or an artistic domain (Bourdieu 1993) – produces observable regularities in individual practices. For Bourdieu, the reason why an academic writes a book, or a consumer decides to buy a particular piece of furniture, is seldom to be found in the subjects' conscious intentions and desires. As Schirato and Roberts note:

> Bourdieu rejects the idea of a knowing, transcendental consciousness (along the lines of the Cartesian cogito) that is separated from and independent of history, social trajectories and cultural frameworks. All activity and knowledge [...] are always informed by a relationship between the agent's history and how this history has been incorporated on the one hand, and their context or circumstances [...] on the other. (Schirato and Roberts 2018: 133–4)

Within this theoretical horizon, free will is reduced to an ideological illusion, and subjects' eventual reflexivity about the social world – such as Bourdieu's own – represents a rare exception to a general 'naturalization' of structural inequalities, cultural norms and social struggles (Bourdieu 1984; Bourdieu and Wacquant 1992). Having said that, the Bourdieusian social world is not as inescapably deterministic as it may seem at first glance. Bourdieu's early accounts of the logic of practice (1977) emphasized individuals' agentic capacity to 'improvise' when confronted with unforeseen experiences, thanks to a 'generative spontaneity' which, nonetheless, works along the lines of action invisibly prescribed by the habitus (King 2000). This socially constrained agentic capacity has been described as practical and pre-conscious (Bourdieu and Wacquant 1992: 22), thus comparable to a jazz pianist's improvisation, whose creativity mainly resides in the contingent, dynamic revisitation of sedimented experiences – scales, phrases, fragments.

According to Wacquant, Bourdieu's 'genetic structuralism' differs, on the one hand, from subjectivist accounts of social action – such as the rational choice paradigm (Coleman 1994) – and, on the other, from an overly 'mechanical structuralism which puts agents "on vacation"' (Bourdieu and Wacquant 1992: 10). Social actors are neither sovereign nor annihilated, but act through a practical 'sense of the game', an 'anticipated adjustment of habitus to the necessities and probabilities inscribed in the field' – which can be easily misinterpreted as subjective will (Bourdieu and Wacquant 1992: 125). It must be acknowledged that a considerable number of scholars have criticized Bourdieu for neglecting social actors' agency and awareness (e.g. King 2000; Jenkins 1993). Notably, these criticisms do not apply to the perfectly unaware and conscienceless agents this book is mainly about.

To a large extent, the automation of the social world is currently delegated to rule-following algorithms with no machine habitus – algorithms that elaborate input data solely through the execution of fixed and formalized commands. Such systems are the foundations of computer software and information networks (McKelvey 2018; Campbell-Kelly et al. 2013). By mechanically actualizing a *deus in machina*, these algorithms act in ways that, sociologically speaking, can be seen as objectively determined (Boudon and Bourricaud 2003: 10). But, again, with the massive implementation of machine learning characterizing the Platform Era, machine agency cannot be wholly reduced to an invariable, mechanical outcome. Socialized machines reason probabilistically, in terms of encoded propensities and situational tendencies (A. Mackenzie 2018; Krasmann 2020), and their practices are often counter-intuitive, mysterious and unexplainable (Campolo and Crawford 2020). That makes artificial social agents like GPT-3 or Google Duplex closer to a jazz pianist than a steam engine. Concretely, this extended machine agency has important consequences for humans: in fact, non-linear, opaque forms of power are ordinarily exerted by the code on the culture.

Computational authority
Toward the end of the 1990s, Google Search's PageRank algorithm began to harvest the entire Web and harness its relational structure in order to automatically produce ranked lists of 'relevant' search results. Existing search engines, like Yahoo, consisted of manually assembled catalogues of websites. At the dawn of the Platform Era, the Internet was still narrated as an uncontaminated cyber-land detached from the interests and inequalities of 'real' life (Orton-Johnson and Prior 2013), and algorithms as abstract mathematical procedures (Chabert 1999). However, a deep change had already been taking place underneath. The Web was turning into an 'electronic marketspace', a vast commercial repository of consumer data and metadata, incessantly retrieved, stored and analysed by the calculative devices built into its networked infrastructure (Zwick and Dholakia 2004; Arvidsson 2004; Ansari, Essegaier and Kohli 2000). Algorithms were mutating into ubiquitous 'engines of order' (Rieder 2020) applied to the organization of culture, information, markets and people (Amoore and Piotukh 2016; Ananny 2016). When platforms like YouTube, Twitter and Facebook made their appearance in the mid 2000s and began the colonization of the entire Internet, this mutation was finally complete.

    As media theorist José van Dijck noted in *The Culture of Connectivity*, '"making the Web social" in reality means "making sociality technical"' (2013: 12). Platform algorithms essentially 'work to determine the new conditions of possibilities of users' lives' (Cheney-Lippold 2011: 167) – as Facebook engineers implicitly acknowledge in the following statement:

> Many of the experiences and interactions people have on Facebook today are made possible with AI. When you log in to Facebook, we use the power of machine learning to provide you with unique, personalized experiences. Machine learning models are part of ranking and personalizing News Feed stories, filtering out offensive content, highlighting trending topics, ranking search results, and much more. (Dunn 2016, cited in A. Mackenzie 2019: 1995)

The critical algorithm studies literature – of which a short overview was given in Chapter 1 – has decisively contributed to the theoretical characterization of this 'social power of algorithms' (Beer 2017). On the one hand, by filtering, pairing and ranking digital content according to opaque computational criteria, algorithms influence the individual actions and experiences of platform users on a large scale, thus limiting human agency (A. Mackenzie 2006: 44; Beer 2013a, 2009; Just and Latzer 2017; Ananny 2016). This first notion of algorithmic power links, for instance, to the impact of microtargeted ads and recommendation systems on consumption patterns (Darmody and Zwick 2020; Gomez-Uribe and Hunt 2015), as well as the various forms of 'programmed sociality' shown by dating apps and social media platforms (Bucher 2012b, 2018; Crawford 2016).

On the other hand, a second conceptualization of the social power of algorithms is, as Neyland argues (2019: 6), of a more Foucauldian kind, and points to the broader consequences of prediction and automation. That is, algorithmic systems are seen as elements in complex webs of dispersed relations jointly producing forms of governmentality which redefine the meaning of knowledge, subjectivity, culture, identity, life, and more (Ziewitz 2016; Amoore and Piotukh 2016; Bucher 2012a). Examples here are the cybernetic remodulation of gender categories by probabilistic models that aim to predict the percentage of 'maleness' of Internet users (Cheney-Lippold 2011), or the notion of 'algorithmic culture' as it has been developed by Striphas (2015) – meaning, 'the use of computational processes to sort, classify, and hierarchize people, places, objects, and ideas, and also the habits of thought, conduct, and expression that arise in relationship to those processes' (Hallinan and Striphas 2016: 119).

In his book *Popular Culture and New Media*, the sociologist David Beer painstakingly articulates how, having become 'a routine part of consumer culture' (2013a: 95), automated systems shape the consumption, taste and 'cultural landscape' of digital users in profound ways. Yet, the power of algorithms extends well beyond online consumption, affecting almost any societal domain where there is a large availability of data. Work is an example – not only in the case of Amazon's warehouses (Delfanti 2019) or app-based services like Uber (Rosenblat and Stark 2016), but, increasingly, across all sectors and organizations. Algorithms are used to control workers in a number of ways, usually characterized by panoptic information asymmetries between controllers and controlled (Crawford et al. 2019; Ajunwa, Crawford and Schultz 2017; Aneesh 2009). A recent paper by Kellogg and colleagues (2020) conceptualizes six main ways in which algorithmic control operates in the workplace: recommending (specific courses of action), restricting (behaviour or access to information), recording (data on employees), rating (performances), replacing (workers, eventually by firing them) and rewarding (activities, also in gamified ways). Moreover, with the widespread delegation of policing and public adminis-tration tasks to automated systems, algorithmic surveillance and power are exerted on citizens too, in addition to workers and consumers (Brayne 2017). This trend is exemplified by the aforementioned use of machine learning software to assess the risk of crime recidivism in the US (Angwin et al. 2016), as well as by the many computational tools regularly employed to manage citizens' access to health care, housing resources and social assistance (Eubanks 2018).

Campolo and Crawford have recently noted that, 'when the disenchanted predictions and classifications of deep learning work as hoped, we see a profusion of optimistic discourse that characterizes these systems as magical, appealing to mysterious forces and superhuman power' (2020: 5). It can be argued that, more than an unspecified power, algorithmic systems hold an *authority* conferred by the mythical discourses on the accuracy and intelligence of automated machines (Beer 2017; Natale and Ballatore 2020; Broussard 2018; Gillespie 2014). It is also on the basis of this computational authority – a blend of the Weberian ideal types of rational-legal and charismatic power, in between disenchantment and magic (Campolo and Crawford 2020) – that more and more traditionally human tasks have been delegated to machines. And it is also because of their recognized legitimacy that algorithms can have tangible effects on the social world, ranging from orienting listeners' taste in music to limiting companies' access to credit.

Interestingly, the possibility of resisting algorithmic control has been rarely discussed in the critical social sciences literature, which so far has tended to portray human subjects as passive and substantially helpless in face of the inscrutable, all-knowing machines of surveillance capitalism (see Velkova and Kaun 2019; Bruns 2019; Neyland 2019). This 'apocalyptic' narrative is certainly not new in the study of media technologies (Eco 1964): eighty years before Cambridge Analytica targeted Facebook users' 'inner demons', it was the capacity of the 'magic bullet' of mass-mediated propaganda to threaten voters' agency and free will that troubled journalists and academics (Rokka and Airoldi 2018; see also Sumpter 2018).

Just as Lazarsfeld and colleagues (1944) empirically rejected this latter, simplistic thesis in the 1940s, recent research has shown how individuals have an active relationship in their encounters with platform-based algorithmic systems. Users may try to figure out how algorithms work in grassroots ways (Siles et al. 2020; Ruckenstein and Granroth 2020); question the functioning of automated systems and the meaning of their outputs – especially when confronted with the errors and failures of algorithmic technologies (Bucher 2017; Kellogg, Valentine and Christin 2020: 390; Summers, Smith and Reczek 2016); or attempt to exploit the computational logics of platforms to their own advantage – like influencers craving more followers on social media, or companies hijacking Google Search's ranks through search engine optimization techniques (Cotter 2019). Eventually, users may even engage in acts of political resistance against the predictions of automated machines (Velkova and Kaun

2019) – as the British students' 'fuck the algorithm' chant
reminded us in 2020. Therefore, as with any other authority,
computational authority emerges from an unstable negoti-
ation. Being in a dialectical relationship with the social
world, it can be contested, and can erode over time (Boudon
and Bourricaud 2003: 39).

These considerations warn us against the risk of overly
deterministic explanations that reduce agents to the
mechanical emanations of powerful social or technological
structures (Bourdieu and Wacquant 1992; MacKenzie and
Wajcman 1999). Society is actively co-produced by the
culturally shaped agencies of socialized humans and machines.
Both operate in ways that affect the actions of the other, generating effects whose echo resonates throughout the interrelated
dimensions of techno-social ecosystems (Rose and Jones 2005).
Both kinds of agents may act on behalf of powerful organizations, such as governments, corporations and platforms
– or they may not, as in the case of IAQOS. An 'intricate
mesh of mutually constitutive agencies' connects artificial
and biological agents within datafied environments (Rieder,
Matamoros-Fernandez and Coromina 2018: 65), together with
their own embodied histories, and (machine) habitus.

Algorithmic distinctions

Concretely, what autonomous machines do is classify reality
(Bechmann and Bowker 2019; Mackenzie 2015; Fourcade
and Johns 2020; Hallinan and Striphas 2016; Ananny 2016).
The code in the culture is deployed to sort images based on
their visual content; products according to their statistical
relatedness; user profiles depending on their creditwor-
thiness, predicted interests or employability; news articles
based on their estimated relevance for specific users. Hence,
the agency and computational authority of algorithms, and,
in particular, of machine learning systems, rest on their
practical ability to draw probabilistically meaningful distinctions among 'objects, people and practices' (Lamont and
Molnár 2002: 168).

Algorithmic distinctions are there for all to see. The machine
learning systems embedded in search engines are designed

to relationally distinguish the relevant from the irrelevant (König and Rasch 2014). Spam filters separate 'spam' from 'ham' and credit scoring models reason analogously in terms of 'loan' and 'not-loan' (Rieder 2017). Recommendation systems map the proximity between items and users, identifying clusters of related products as well as of customers sharing similar tastes and consumption habits (Prey 2018). Platforms computationally produce 'calculated publics' selectively exposed to 'filter bubbles' of content tailored to their estimated behavioural categories (Crawford 2016; Pariser 2011). Hence, implemented as means to efficiently order 'the masses of digital and datafied bits and pieces that clutter the environments we inhabit' (Rieder 2020: 10), algorithms end up dividing culture and society into fuzzy, ephemeral classes (Cheney-Lippold 2017), through categorical logics acquired from social data.

Algorithmic judgements produce social distinctions (Bourdieu 1984), even when they are designed to personalize users' intimate digital experiences based on local data contexts. For machines, individuals exist only as everchanging collections of data points (Cheney-Lippold 2011; 2017). Their encoded propensities are always 'impersonal' (A. Mackenzie 2018): what matters is not the classified subject, but the datafied features that allow this particular subject to be situated in a multidimensional vector space, closer to someone and further from someone else, at a given point in time (Darmody and Zwick 2020; Prey 2018). The output of calculations segments society *horizontally*, in terms of similarities and differences, as well as *vertically*, through ratings, scores and prioritizations. Fourcade and Johns (2020) call these two ideal types of machine classification, respectively, 'nominal' and 'ordinal', also arguing that they are rooted in pre-digital social hierarchies and struggles. Indeed, machine categorizations do not operate in a socio-cultural vacuum, nor do they consist of mere statistical artefacts detached from social reality (Campolo and Crawford 2020: 15). The previous chapter illustrated how machine learning systems' practical reason is itself the product of repeated human classifications: those made by machine creators, crystallized as *deus in machina*, as well as those made by machine trainers, inscribed in the data patterns forming

the machine habitus. ImageNet, a popular training dataset
including over 4 million labelled images organized into more
than 20,000 categories, well exemplifies the very human
categorizations employed in machine learning:

> As we go further into the depths of ImageNet's Person
> categories, the classifications of humans within it take a sharp
> and dark turn. There are categories for Bad Person, Call Girl,
> Drug Addict, Closet Queen, Convict, Crazy, Failure, Flop,
> Fucker, Hypocrite, Jezebel, Kleptomaniac, Loser, Melancholic,
> Nonperson, Pervert, Prima Donna, Schizophrenic, Second-
> Rater, Spinster, Streetwalker, Stud, Tosser, Unskilled Person,
> Wanton, Waverer, and Wimp. There are many racist slurs and
> misogynistic terms. (Crawford and Paglen 2019)

Sociologists have been studying classification systems for
a long time (Bowker and Star 1999; Lamont and Molnár
2002; DiMaggio 1987). The interiorized ways in which
we, as humans, sort reality and experiences into categorical
boxes are culturally and institutionally fabricated in ways
that reflect power relations (Berger and Luckmann 1966;
Bourdieu 1990a). This is the case, for instance, with language,
which objectifies historical distinctions between oppressed
and oppressors, as in the case of female and masculine terms
in French, Spanish or Italian. That vast anthropological
matter called 'culture' largely consists of socially shared,
ever-changing systems of classification which determine the
'standards of morality and excellence' for 'judging the others
as well as oneself' (Barth 1981: 203). At the same time, 'the
manner in which culture has been acquired lives on in the
manner of using it' (Bourdieu 1984: 3), meaning that the
classificatory schemes acquired through socialization are then
unwittingly reproduced by the practices of social agents.

Machine learning algorithms are not an exception to this
sociological rule: the culture in the code informs the classificatory practices of the code in the culture (Mackenzie 2015;
Fourcade and Johns 2020). The social distinctions computed
by a deep learning system trained on ImageNet may well
include the one between 'Call Girl' and 'Prima Donna'. These
categories have no intrinsic meaning for the machine, other
than a varying statistical configuration of pixels. Nonetheless,
machine-learned associations between aggregated pixels and

labels derive from human trainers' practices and 'classificatory imagination' (Beer 2013b).

While being 'ordinarily invisible' (Bowker and Star 1999: 2), classification systems have huge consequences for the lives of people. Belonging to the 'wrong' ethnicity, caste, gender or social class implies material inequalities and stigmatizations. The horizontal and vertical distinctions among groups and social strata often link to symbolic boundaries between 'us' and 'them', which tend to 'enforce, maintain, normalize, or rationalize' underlying social structures (Lamont and Molnár 2002:186). The enactment of algorithmic classifications – and misclassifications – has equally important social implications. Not solely because, as we have seen already, automated systems often make hard-to-detect mistakes, unfairly discriminate between individuals and social groups, and arbitrarily limit their access to services and resources (Eubanks 2018; O'Neil 2016; Broussard 2018). On top of that, as machines are increasingly in charge of filtering and ranking the social world, they have become directly involved in the cultural (re)production of classification systems and symbolic boundaries – as Noble's work clearly shows:

> the Internet is both reproducing social relations and creating new forms of relations based on our engagement with it. Technologies and their design do not dictate racial ideologies; rather, they reflect the current climate. As users engage with technologies such as search engines, they dynamically co-construct content and the technology itself. (Noble 2018: 151)

The techno-social interplay recursively linking the classificatory practices of humans and machines is particularly visible in platformized cultural markets. Today, recommendation systems are probably more influential in guiding the circulation and reception of music, movies, podcasts and TV series than are human cultural intermediaries such as critics, producers and journalists (Morris 2015; Bonini and Gandini 2019; Beer 2013a; Gillespie 2014). On streaming platforms like Spotify, Netflix or YouTube, the 'presentation and representation' of cultural goods, and the drawing of 'analogies endlessly pointing to other analogies' (Bourdieu 1984: 53) that have traditionally defined the editorial work of professional tastemakers, are to a large extent delegated to recommender algorithms (Hallinan and Striphas 2016; Webster 2019). A well-known example is Spotify's 'Discover Weekly', a hybrid recommendation system whose operational functioning is described by Prey as follows:

> Discover Weekly first combs through its massive collection of playlists to find lists that include the songs and artists you love. While Discover Weekly incorporates both professionally curated playlists and the roughly 2 billion user-generated playlists in its algorithm, it gives more weight to playlists with more followers and to Spotify-generated playlists [...]. Next, it identifies the songs on those playlists that you have not heard. Finally, it filters those songs through your own Taste Profile, in order to only select the undiscovered songs that match the particular type of music fan that you are. (Prey 2018: 1091)

The ongoing transition toward an 'automation of taste' (Barile and Sugiyama 2015) is likely to impact cultural fields on different levels. At the level of user experience, algorithmic distinctions such as those leading to the prioritization of Kendrick Lamar tracks and the concomitant disappearance of Serge Gainsbourg from my Discover Weekly have the straightforward effect of orienting listening habits – in this case, toward the rap artist. If this happens on a regular basis, then my actual taste and consumption practices become, in fact, computational by-products of algorithmic propensities acquired from my past behavioural traces (Cheney-Lippold 2017; Beer 2013a; Prey 2018; Barile and Sugiyama 2015). There is more: if we zoom out and consider the macro level of culture, the accumulation of myriad user-level feedback loops such as the one above is likely to contribute to the transformation of artistic classification systems, through the renegotiation of the socially shared categorical boundaries defining genre categories and artistic hierarchies (Airoldi 2021; Airoldi, Beraldo and Gandini 2016; DiMaggio 1987; Beer 2013a).

From the perspective of a single user, the recommender system assigned to each Spotify account works as a full-time gatekeeper, along with the human curators designing playlists and content strategies (Bonini and Gandini 2019; Webster

2019). It has a cultural – yet computational – authority, exerted through the ever-changing musical selections tailored to (predicted) preferences (Prey 2018). Whether individual or computational, taste 'classifies, and classifies the classifier' (Bourdieu 1984: 6); that is, by practically distinguishing between 'the beautiful and the ugly', the artificial social agent implicitly reveals the social origins of its probabilistic distinctions – rooted in the local and global data contexts of machine socialization. Most likely, in line with Bourdieu's original account of the logic of cultural distinction, the path-dependent classificatory practices of machine learning systems will reflect pre-existing social divisions and relations of symbolic power (1984; 1989a) – making it more probable, for instance, that those musical forms recognized as 'legitimate' in a given context will be recommended to 'distinguished' users already accustomed to them (Fourcade and Johns 2020). Alternatively, these systems may also help consumers emancipating themselves from their social background and habitus, discovering new content and, thus, building cultural capital (Webster 2019: 2; Beer 2013a: 95–6).

While empirical evidences demonstrate that algorithmic distinctions significantly influence individual choice (Gomez-Uribe and Hunt 2015; Jiang et al. 2019; Hargreaves et al., 2018; Wu, Rizoiu and Xie 2019), their second-order consequences on society and culture are harder to estimate. In theory, one could expect that, as multiple computational models analyse the social world, the social world swiftly responds to predictions, in a recursive circle (Kitchin and Dodge 2011: 30). However, 'the concrete forms of action and transformation that might take shape in relation to machine learning are not yet obvious' (Mackenzie 2015: 443; see also Rahwan et al. 2019; Fourcade and Johns 2020). For instance, empirical studies addressing the hypothesized causal relation between algorithmic filter bubbles and a rampant political polarization have produced contrasting results so far (for a critical review, see Bruns 2019). In order to reflect sociologically on the complex feedback loops between the code and the culture, my analytical strategy consists in first zooming in, getting closer to where socialized machines interact.

How socialized machines interact

More-than-human relations

Just as human existence is compenetrated by cultural, biological and material elements such as air, water, bacteria and ideas, the everyday life of an algorithm is entangled with networked infrastructures made of computer code, protocols, hardware and data. These ramified techno-social ecosystems are inhabited by vast populations of autonomous machines, mostly hidden in the depths, behind our user-friendly interfaces. In the ventilated rooms of data centres and server farms, densely wired racks of computers host more-than-human relations: high-frequency trading algorithms compete for the best price on largely automated financial markets; real-time-bidding systems auction online advertising spaces within milliseconds; crypto-mining algorithms dig bitcoins up by solving mathematical puzzles; AI content moderation tools flag the outputs of spammy social bots, while bias detection systems police AI models at runtime (D. MacKenzie 2019; Burr, Cristianini and Ladyman 2018; Mellet and Beauvisage 2020; Gillespie 2018; Bessi and Ferrara 2016; Tsvetkova et al. 2017; Jiang and Nachum 2020).

Rahwan and colleagues (2019) have portrayed these artificial agents as animals in the wild, engaging in one-to-one interactions and forms of collective behaviour. However, isolating an algorithmic system from its techno-social habitat is not as straightforward as it may seem. The anthropologist Nick Seaver has cleverly remarked that 'algorithms are not technical rocks in a cultural stream, but are rather just more water' (2017: 5). They are not 'singular technical objects that enter into many different cultural interactions, but rather unstable objects' which are embedded in – and, somehow, inseparable from – complex socio-technical assemblages (Gillespie 2016).

Still, just as we normally treat humans and animals as individual agents at once independent from and related to the air they breathe, the partners they mate with and the bacteria they have, so we can see each algorithmic program as a recognizable artificial entity related to other human and non-human entities – which is what AI researchers, developers and even users tend to do (Science Magazine 2018; Harrison 2018; Siles et al. 2020; Gillespie 2014). This perspective is widely shared in the social sciences and humanities (e.g. Burr, Cristianini and Ladyman 2018; Esposito 2017; Knorr Cetina 2009; Floridi and Sanders 2004; see also Cerulo 2009), and it has been developed in sociology by the STS scholar Donald MacKenzie.

Taking inspiration from Knorr Cetina's work, MacKenzie has recently argued that Erving Goffman's classic theories of social interaction can be extended 'to situations in which trading algorithms interact with each other rather than human beings' (2019: 41). In the highly digitalized domain of financial markets, most of the work is done by autonomous machines, employed to place and match orders, predict price movements and deceive competing algorithms (D. MacKenzie 2018; 2019; O'Neil 2016; Pardo-Guerra 2010). Notwithstanding their 'silicon bodies', purely instrumental goals and total lack of consciousness, thousands of artificial agents working for high-frequency trading firms co-produce an 'interaction order' that, according to MacKenzie, presents communicative strategies and forms of collective organiz-ation which resemble the face-to-face situations famously observed by Goffman (1983). Nonhuman interactions are also somehow shaped by social institutions – such as financial regulations – and material arrangements such as the length of the fibre cables connecting servers, which physically affects the speed of automated interactions and, therefore, their success (D. MacKenzie 2018; 2019). These opaque data-based exchanges can potentially have very tangible effects on the social world, as the following example of an algorithmi-cally induced 'flash crash' in the stock markets shows:

@AP: Breaking: Two Explosions in the White House and Barack Obama is injured. This message appeared on Tuesday, 23 April 2013, at 1.07 pm ET on the official Associated Press Twitter account @AP. It quickly received over 4000 retweets and a number of favorites. Within seconds, according to the Reuters data, the Dow Jones Industrial Average dropped 143.5 points, and nearly $136.5 billion of the Standard & Poor's 500 Index's value was wiped out. [...] The tweet was revealed as the result of a malicious hack of the Associated Press Twitter account. The recovery of the markets was rapid.

Just as quickly as the announcement of the explosions had led to a precipitous drop, the market had returned to its former position. The entire event happened in less than five minutes. (Karppi and Crawford 2016: 2)

The interaction order of algorithms can be observed also outside of financial markets. A large fraction of the user base of social media platforms like Twitter and Facebook is composed of 'social bots' sharing news and posting content, whose coordinated actions are believed to have significantly affected public opinion dynamics during multiple electoral campaigns (Bessi and Ferrara 2016; Giglietto et al. 2020). The allocation of online advertising spaces is ordinarily accomplished through real-time auctions happening within the time taken by a webpage to load, with the aim of determining which advertiser is willing to pay the most for their advertisement to be shown to a specific user profile (Burr, Cristianini and Ladyman 2018:737; Mellet and Beauvisage 2020). Moreover, beneath the digital surface of the World Wide Web, 'in every router, switch, and hub', algorithmic 'daemons' jointly orchestrate the global flows of digital information, determining the speed of your Zoom call and file sharing (McKelvey 2018: 67).

Regardless of the encoded prescriptions of the *deus in machina*, human-free algorithmic interactions can lead to unexpected outcomes. These are not necessarily due to a twisted machine training, as in the examples discussed in the previous chapter, but more often result from complex interactional dynamics. For instance, through an analysis of all the interactions among editing bots that occurred on Wikipedia between 2001 and 2010, Tsvetkova and colleagues highlighted how these systems 'behave and interact as unpredictably and as inefficiently as the humans' (2017: 7). A sizeable portion of Wikipedia entries are edited by autonomous bots which, at the time of the research, were mainly employed to link different language editions. The study found that these relatively simple rule-following machines tended to disagree with each other, and engaged in fights over specific entries, often prolonged over years. Today, Wikipedia editors can employ more sophisticated machine learning tools trained on human-labelled data, with the aim of reviewing potentially damaging contributions (Halfaker et al. 2018).

It can be argued that, within the layered techno-social environments of the Internet, the interaction orders of humans and machines blend (D. MacKenzie 2019; Rahwan et al. 2019). In order to exchange with each other, billions of platform users – knowingly or not – first and foremost interact with an even higher number of individually tailored algorithmic systems, incessantly mediating and modulating interpersonal communications, markets, romantic relations, public opinion, and social life more broadly. Myriad feedback loops allow users and machine learning systems to learn from each other, thus reshaping each other's actions – along with society as a whole (Fourcade and Johns 2020). In the following pages, I will discuss how these recursive processes and their effects may vary in relation to different types of interactional configuration.

Informational asymmetry and cultural alignment

What does the future hold for recommendations? We believe there's more opportunity ahead of us than behind us. We imagine intelligent interactive services where shopping is as easy as a conversation. This moves beyond the current paradigm of typing search keywords in a box and navigating a website. Instead, discovery should be like talking with a friend who knows you, knows what you like, works with you at every step, and anticipates your needs. This is a vision where intelligence is everywhere. Every interaction should reflect who you are and what you like, and help you find what other people like you have already discovered.

This is how Amazon's Brent Smith and Greg Linden from Microsoft imagined the evolution of interactions between intelligent machines and platform users (2017: 17–18). At first glance, it seems that we, the humans, are in control. After all, the recommender system smoothly adjusts its outputs to our needs and desires. However, a closer reading of the excerpt tells us something different: the artificial 'friend' Smith and Linden talk about knows everything about us, while we know nothing about it; it is 'everywhere', anticipates what we want, and leverages this knowledge in 'every interaction'; also, 'moving beyond' search and navigation essentially means taking out any residual proactivity by platform users, transforming them (us) even further into passive receivers of 'positive reminders resulting from specific information processing tasks' (Striphas 2015: 406). Hence, this imagined human–machine interaction is authoritatively orchestrated by the machine learning system, which is programmed to exploit the informational capital accumulated during its data-driven socialization, in pursuit of the unilateral commercial goals of the platform.

The future sketched by Smith and Linden is already here. It is the same techno-optimistic scenario announced at Google I/O 2018 by Sundar Pichai. Its logics and technical seeds lie in the versions of Google Search, Facebook, Amazon and Netflix that we navigate on a daily basis. Yet, platform-driven encounters of the kind envisioned above are only one out of several possible configurations of human–machine relations. Alternative types of interaction can ideally take place, where the circulation of information between algorithms and users is more horizontal and less black-boxed. Furthermore, users' contingent interests and expectations may be more or less aligned with the encoded goals and propensities of the socialized machines they encounter every day. In fact, while Spotify's recommendations might perfectly fit my current musical taste, content selection on Facebook may annoyingly prioritize the posts of some forgotten school friends, and behaviourally targeted ads dumbly insist on products I have already purchased (Bucher 2017). These marginal differences in human–machine interactions do make a difference in the ways and the extent to which machine learning systems participate in society and impact on it.

According to Burr and colleagues, all interactions between users and 'intelligent software agents' (ISAs) – that is, socialized machines incorporated in digital environments – follow a recursive script:

(1) The ISA has to choose from a set of available actions that bring about interaction with the user. For example, recommending a video or news item; suggesting an exercise in a tutoring task; displaying a set of products and prices, and perhaps also the context, layout, order and timing with which

to present them. (2) The user chooses an action, thereby revealing information about their knowledge and preferences to the controlling agent. [...] (3) The cycle repeats resulting in a process of feedback and learning. (Burr, Cristianini and Ladyman 2018: 736)

Here I argue that, depending on the contingent combination of two main dimensions – that is, high/low *informational asymmetry* and strong/weak *cultural alignment* – the recursive interactions between humans and machines can assume four main ideal-typical configurations, which will be illustrated in the following section.

First, let me clarify what I mean by informational asymmetry. In the near totality of their digitally mediated interactions, artificial agents have more information on users' behaviour than users have on the agents' algorithmic functioning. In the critical literature, opacity and inscrutability have been indicated as constitutive features of algorithms and AI technologies (Burrell 2016; Dourish 2016; Pasquale 2015; Campolo and Crawford 2020; Cardon 2018; Bucher 2012a; Beer 2009). According to the programmer, artist and activist Denis Roio, 'while we see a growth of the possibilities to harvest data from "smart environments", while sensors proliferate in public and private spaces, there is limited knowledge on how to understand the algorithms that process such data', also due to 'proprietary barriers from the very access to such algorithms' (2018: 54). Even though bottom-up attempts to reverse-engineer the black-boxed computational logics governing human–machine interactions regularly take place (Siles et al. 2020; Bucher 2017), the exact formulation of the code is changeable and largely 'immune from scrutiny' (Pasquale 2015: 5). Artificial agents, on their part, are fed with as much updated information as possible about users' local data contexts (Fourcade and Johns 2020). When a machine learning system starts interacting with a recently registered user, its initial predictions rely on little or no information – an issue known in computer science as a 'cold start problem' (Celma 2010; Seaver 2019). The longer its secondary machine socialization is, the more informational capital the algorithm accumulates, and the wider the informational asymmetry gets.

The degree of informational asymmetry also depends on the digital literacy of the human in the loop (Burrell 2016). Klawitter and Hargittai concluded their qualitative research on entrepreneurs' understandings of automated systems by arguing that 'algorithms are very hard to grasp for people [...]. Algorithmic skills remain the domain of a select few users, even among the most highly motivated' (2018: 3505). A recent study by Gran and colleagues (2020) has shown that Norwegian Internet users' level of awareness and understanding of platform algorithms are strongly associated to socio-demographic factors, as happens with other digital skills (Hargittai and Micheli 2019; Lutz 2019). More specifically, older, female and lower-educated respondents living outside urban areas were significantly more likely to have low or even no awareness of their ubiquitous interactions with artificial agents. Such discrepancies are likely to be even broader in poorer and less digitalized countries. When characterized by a lack of 'algorithmic awareness' on the part of the users (Gran, Booth and Bucher 2020), human–machine interactions take on the asymmetric configuration of a 'technological unconscious' invisibly governing digital experiences (Beer 2009).

Far from being natural or inevitable, informational asymmetries are an in-built characteristic of the deliberately panoptic architecture of for-profit apps and platforms (Rosenblat and Stark 2016; Ruckenstein and Granroth 2020; Cheney-Lippold 2017). Reducing them is one of the political rationales behind the open-source code of IAQOS, which has been designed to allow its interlocutors to – literally – see what the AI system thinks in real time (Iaconesi and Persico 2019). The same intent of creating a more horizontal circulation of information between calculative devices and their classified users has driven other projects at the intersection of art, activism and research, such as DataSelfie.it (Hang 2018) – a browser extension simulating Facebook's predictive surveillance in order to make it visible and increase algorithmic awareness – or the free software Dowse, defined by one of its creators as 'a smart digital network appliance [...] that makes it possible to connect objects and people in a friendly, conscious and responsible manner' (Roio 2018: 54). If it is evident that a high informational asymmetry currently represents the norm in human–machine relations, instances of low information asymmetry exist too.

A second relevant interactional dimension regards the strength of the cultural alignment between machine learning systems and their users at a given moment in time. Value alignment is considered 'one of the top priorities in AI research', and is broadly intended as the adaptation of algorithmic functioning to users' specific values and preferences – for instance, through personalization (Kim, Donaldson and Hooker 2018; Burr, Cristianini and Ladyman 2018: 761). Here I reframe this computer science problem sociologically in terms of alignment between the *cultures in and outside the code*, that is, between users' habitus and machine habitus.

For Bourdieu, 'the truth of the interaction is never entirely contained in the interaction'.

> Every confrontation between agents in fact brings together, in an interaction [...] systems of dispositions (carried by 'natural persons') such as linguistic competence and a cultural competence and, through these habitus, all the objective structures of which they are the product [...] interpersonal relations are never, except in appearance, individual-to-individual relationships. (Bourdieu 1990a: 81)

The mediation of the habitus also characterizes human–machine interactions, at both ends. On the part of the users, all 'external stimuli and conditioning experiences' – including platform-based ones – 'are, at every moment, perceived through categories already constructed by prior experience' (Bourdieu and Wacquant 1992: 13). For Bourdieu, this experiential structuring of perceptions and expectations works as a sort of 'patterned inertia', which inclines agents to appreciate the familiar more than the 'unthinkable' and the unknown (1977: 77). For instance, while the automated recommendation of a free jazz tune might be perceived as 'too difficult' by an unhabituated ear, a generational pop hit could sound reassuringly pleasant (Bourdieu 1984). Similarly, machine learning algorithms are path-dependent (Mackenzie 2015), as they read unseen data contexts through the encoded propensities of the machine habitus. A system may struggle, at first, 'to find the proper level of familiarity, novelty and relevance for each user', even more so given that these change over time (Celma 2010: 7). Through accretive, feedback-based learning, artificial social agents attempt mimetically to adjust their global practices and dispositions to the local data contexts of their users. Still, despite all these efforts, habitus and machine habitus can never exactly coincide, due to the necessarily imperfect epistemic translation of social reality into data contexts (see Chapter 2). As a result, such cybernetic alignments often turn out to be manifestly inaccurate, as in the following example reported by Bucher:

> In the past, Kayla has posted on Facebook about being broke and single. She had to cancel her gym membership (Facebook seems to constantly remind her of this) and she has used dating apps to find a potential partner. Recently, Kayla has been looking at nursery decorations online for a baby shower gift. As she scrolls down her news feed, she notices how the algorithm for suggested apps shows her multiple dating sites and multiple pregnancy-related apps in the same set of suggestions. How bizarre. On Twitter, she notes how Facebook seems to think that she is 'pregnant, single, broke and should lose weight'. Tellingly, Kayla adds, 'the Facebook algorithm confuses me'. (Bucher 2017: 34)

Kayla's experience is an instance of cultural misalignment between human and machine, leading to the computational misrecognition of the user. Another participant in the same study similarly described her Facebook newsfeed as 'out of sync with her interests and beliefs' (Bucher 2017: 35). Yet, the feedback loop connecting the embodied dispositions of platform users and machine learning systems usually leads, over time, to a more or less stable cultural alignment. This eventually produces an apparent 'naturalization' of the computational authority – which, as a result, 'remains imperceptible to those whose data traces are being used' (Ruckenstein and Granroth 2020: 3).

Cases of misalignment can also originate whenever developers' goals inscribed as *deus in machina* clash with the user's will and utility (Kim, Donaldson and Hooker 2018). For instance, this occurs in consumers' interactions with pricing algorithms employed by airlines, railway companies or hotels, which are programmed to maximize revenues at the expense of the user (Burr, Cristianini and Ladyman 2018: 748). Here the machine is designed not to collaborate, but to (unfairly) compete with humans by exploiting informational asymmetries. Notably, unlike the weak cultural alignment originating from a transitory lack of data or an unsuccessful machine socialization, such a misalignment by design is irreversible.

A typology of user–machine interactions
By considering at once variations in the degree of informational asymmetry (IA) and in the strength of cultural alignment (CA), I can derive four ideal types of interactional configuration, characterized by different algorithmic roles and emerging outcomes. These are summarized in Table 2, as well as described below:

(1) *Assisting*. When user–machine relations have a high IA and a strong CA, users do not know or even notice the computational logics in play, but feel anyway satisfied and *at ease* with their outputs. This is by far tech companies' favourite scenario (Smith and Linden 2017). The machine learning system smoothly *assists* the interacting user, by selecting familiar content comfortably aligned with her tacit expectations. The user reacts by (unknowingly) sending a positive behavioural feedback to the machine – for instance, by watching or liking a recommended video – thus *reinforcing* the encoded cultural propensities displayed by the system in a new iteration. This way, in interaction after interaction, the assisted users are also likely to see a *reinforcement* of their pre-existing opinions, social relations, habits and habitus (Burr, Cristianini and Ladyman 2018: 754; Jiang et al. 2019) – as has been widely theorized by the critical literature on filter bubbles, search engines and social media (Pariser 2011; Bozdag 2013; Hallinan and Striphas 2016; Beer 2013b; Bucher 2012a). An empirical study conducted by Hargreaves and colleagues (2018) during the 2018 electoral campaign in Italy helps illustrate this point. The authors created six artificial Facebook users and attributed distinct political orientations to each of them, operationalized through differential patterns of page likes. For nearly three months,

the six undercover bots collected snapshots of the personalized content proposed in the newsfeed, demonstrating
that the opaque platform algorithm tended to 'reinforce
the orientation indicated by users' through the systematic
prioritization of posts from politically aligned sources.
The habitus-driven algorithmic distinctions separating the
relevant from the irrelevant, the visible from the invisible,
significantly reduce users' digital options, pushing them to
interact with the tailored filtered content. This way, the
machine's outputs alter the datafied context of its feedback-
based learning, 'confounding' its input data (Chaney, Stewart
and Engelhardt 2018) and iteratively reinforcing the user's
comfortable filter bubble.

(2) *Nudging*. A high IA and a weak CA generate an unbalanced interactional situation where the user is oriented by an
invisible computational authority against her own inclinations or will. Having a minimal algorithmic awareness, the
user barely notices that a technological force is exerted on her.
The machine behaves according to encoded logics partially
independent from the ones guiding the user, either because of
a lack of local training, or due to deliberate design choices.
In the first case, repeated negative feedback on the part of the
user – for instance, a skipped recommendation or removed
ad – can somehow adjust the machine habitus and produce
a gradual cultural realignment – as in the case of the aforementioned 'cold start' problem (Celma 2010). Otherwise,
and until then, the system opaquely *nudges* the user's actions,
potentially inducing some sort of behavioural *transformation*.
Here I use the term 'nudge' to indicate algorithmic outputs
capable of deviating users from their habitual conduct or
way of thinking. Machine learning systems ordinarily nudge
platform users through micro-targeted ads, notifications and
recommendations, often giving rise to forms of manipulation,
regimentation and gamified control (Kellogg, Valentine and
Christin 2020; Christin 2020; Darmody and Zwick 2020).
The nudge-based exercise of computational authority is
particularly effective when users are workers rather than
consumers – as in the case of Uber drivers, who cannot
simply ignore algorithmic control, since the murky algorithm
is the boss (Rosenblat and Stark 2016). Nudge after nudge,

the machine 'might end up changing not only the user's immediate actions (e.g. whether to share a news article, or watch a video) but also long-term attitudes and beliefs, simply by controlling the exposure of a user to certain types of content' (Burr, Cristianini and Ladyman 2018: 745). After a prolonged trip into the 'rabbit hole' of YouTube's related videos, we might re-emerge 'radicalized', since 'our tastes adjust' to more and more extreme content – argued Tufekci (2018) in the *New York Times*. Still, algorithmic nudging is not necessarily bad for the user: in fact, it could also represent a chance to burst the pre-digital cultural bubble produced by the habitus' *amor fati* – that is, the love for the familiar resulting from the interiorization of social structures (Lizardo 2013). While this social inertia is technologically reinforced by aligned machines *assisting* users, misaligned relations have 'the potential to detach the formation of taste from class-related socialisation' (Webster 2019: 2) – for instance, by nudging a working-class consumer toward the accumulation of a middle-class cultural capital, consisting of 'legitimate' movies, books or records (Bourdieu 1984).

(3) *Collaborating.* The case of an interactional configuration characterized by a low IA and a strong CA is not very common in the platform society. It implies a horizontal circulation of information between an algorithmically aware user and a successfully socialized machine, which is responsive to the user's datafied inclinations. A major difference with respect to the previous two ideal types is that, in this case, the machine learning system does not need to spy on us in order to accumulate data traces: the 'sovereign' users can willingly provide the explicit feedback necessary to produce an effective personalization (Reviglio and Agosti 2020; Roio 2018). Apart from the rare, aforementioned cases of open-source AI technologies developed with the purpose of challenging platforms' exploitative logics, such a human–machine *collaboration* can currently take place only when the user and the machine creator are the same person. This is not as unlikely as one might think. In fact, thanks to a multiplication of available resources, often developed by the same tech companies benefiting from platform surveillance – Google's TensorFlow is a well-known

example – machine learning tools are increasingly easy to build, even for beginners. For instance, I could potentially build from scratch a neural-network-based chatbot trained on my past social media conversations, and use it to answer Facebook messages on my behalf, thanks to the Python code kindly shared online by Deshpande (2017). The outcome of this third ideal type of user–machine interaction is then a transparent *co-production* of value.

(4) *Misunderstanding.* In order to realize that something is not working as expected, one must be aware that there is something going on, and at least have some vague knowledge about it. As we have seen in the case of *nudging*, this is not always the case. However, moments of misalignment are also occasions for digitally skilled platform users to gain algorithmic awareness, and thus partially counterbalance the usual informational asymmetries (Ruckenstein and Granroth 2020; Gran, Booth and Bucher 2020). This is the case of inter-actions characterized by a low IA and weak CA. Repeated algorithmic failures, such as 'out of sync' recommendations or clearly 'deceiving' micro-targeted ads, can foster the bottom-up questioning of machine learning technologies (Bucher 2017; Burr, Cristianini and Ladyman 2018; Siles et al. 2020). Hence, the likely interactional outcome of a machine systematically *misunderstanding* an aware user is a *disillusionment* on her part (Ruckenstein and Granroth 2020: 11), which substantially undermines the continuity of the interaction and, therefore, the successful exercise of compu-tational authority. This disillusionment may subsequently lead to a (partial) disconnection from the medium (Bucher 2020) and, eventually, to organized forms of 'algorithmic resistance' (Velkova and Kaun 2019).

It should be noted that these ideal types of user–machine interaction correspond, for the most part, to transitory states that may vary over time, depending on the trajectory of the participating agents. Furthermore, my non-exhaustive typology focuses on relations where the algorithmically classified subject corresponds to the interacting user – this, however, is not always the case (Christin 2020: 1128). In fact, the datafied subject of algorithmic classifications could also

Table 2 Types of user–machine interaction (effects on users in brackets)

	High informational asymmetry	Low informational asymmetry
Strong alignment	*Assisting* (reinforcement)	*Collaborating* (co-production)
Weak alignment	*Nudging* (transformation)	*Misunderstanding* (disillusionment)

be a traveller passing by an airport-based intelligent surveillance camera (Neyland 2019), a candidate applying for a job at Amazon (Dastin 2018), or a homeless person whose chances of receiving housing may depend on an automated process (Eubanks 2018). In all these cases, the user interacting *directly* with the machine is the employee of an organization – a security officer, a HR manager, a social worker – thanks to whom the artificial agent refines the arbitrary probabilistic criteria for distinguishing a 'suspect terrorist', a 'promising applicant' or a 'needy person'. When relations with the machine learning algorithm are *indirect*, as they are for the unaware targets of data surveillance, the informational asymmetry is at its maximum, and so, arguably, is the computational authority exerted by the classifying machine.

Platforms as techno-social fields

Encapsulating and confounding
We are heading toward the end of this chapter, and it is time to zoom out with our imaginary camera. The interacting users and machines of the previous section should now look like thousands of small dots connected by thin lines – such as those in Figure 4 below. From this panoramic point of view, it is easier to see how digital platforms 'may be likened to fields in the Bourdieusian sense' (Fourcade and Johns 2020; see also Levina and Arriaga 2014).

Inspired by the philosopher Ernst Cassirer, Bourdieu saw the real as relational: any element of social life will be defined by the latent systems of relations within which all elements

are contained (Kirchner and Mohr 2010). Bourdieu called
these relational systems 'fields' (1983, 1989a, 1993, 2002).
The value of a novel is inseparable from the historically
contingent configuration of the literary field; a 'legitimate'
US presidential speech in 2020 would have been 'unimaginable' according to the common sense (or *doxa*) of the same
political field in 1990; my academic carrier is evaluated each
year in relation to the accomplishments of other scholars
in my field; ultimately, every individual and organizational
endeavour is structurally entangled with the historically
determined relational dynamics characterizing the social and
symbolic layers of intersecting fields.

According to Bourdieu, these are essentially 'battlefields'
(Bourdieu and Wacquant 1992: 17), spaces of conflict and
competition among agents investing economic, social and
cultural capital to improve their relative positions of power
and status (Bourdieu 1986). Like games, fields have taken-
for-granted rules, such as the academic 'publish or perish'
and the neoliberal 'get rich or die trying'. Like players, social
agents possess a practical 'sense of the game', are organized
in teams, and are committed to winning. They have interiorized the rules but can still somehow improvise (Bourdieu
and Wacquant 1992: 22; Schirato and Roberts 2018: 156).

Digital platforms deliberately aim to encapsulate the fields
of social life (Helmond 2015; Cotter 2019; A. Mackenzie
2019; van Dijck 2013). Our social capital is roughly indicated
by the number of friends we have on Facebook or followers
on Instagram; the symbolic capital of restaurants, hotels and
museums is crystallized in the popularity rankings and user-
generated reviews featured on TripAdvisor, Yelp, Booking.
com, and the like; LinkedIn quantifies its users' professional
status and network, while the metrics assigned to scholars in
ResearchGate further gamify scientific production. We have
all intuitively experienced how this process of platformization works, and how pervasive it is. Since platforms
are conceived as information networks linking consumers,
brands, content and producers, they subsume the relational
dynamism of Bourdieu's abstract fields, making it visible
as well as better trackable – to the delight of digital
ethnographers and computational social scientists (Salganik
2018). However, this encapsulation is anything but the neutral

process of disintermediation portrayed in techno-optimistic and business-driven discourses: in reality, 'a platform is a mediator rather than an intermediary: it shapes the performance of social acts instead of merely facilitating them' (van Dijck 2013: 29).

More than simply translating fields into data, platforms engineer field-specific social struggles and relations in order to extract economic value (Zuboff 2019; van Dijck, Poell and de Waal 2018; Beer 2016; Gerlitz and Helmond 2013). In his book *Bit by Bit: Social Research in the Digital Age*, the computational sociologist Matthew Salganik remarks how 'digital systems that record behavior are highly engineered to induce specific behaviors such as clicking on ads or posting content'. He calls this phenomenon 'algorithmic confounding', and illustrates it with the following example:

> on Facebook there are an anomalously high number of users with approximately 20 friends, as was discovered by Johan Ugander and colleagues (2011). Scientists analyzing this data without any understanding of how Facebook works could doubtless generate many stories about how 20 is some kind of magical social number. Fortunately, Ugander and his colleagues had a substantial understanding of the process that generated the data, and they knew that Facebook encouraged people with few connections on Facebook to make more friends until they reached 20 friends. Although Ugander and colleagues don't say this in their paper, this policy was presumably created by Facebook in order to encourage new users to become more active. In other words, the surprisingly high number of people with about 20 friends tells us more about Facebook than about human behavior. (Salganik 2018: 35)

On the one hand, we have seen how the *culture in the code* is imbued with the logics of the platformized fields where machine learning systems are applied and socialized. Chatbots like Microsoft's Tay learn how to tweet from Twitter users (Desole 2020), Facebook's EdgeRank absorbs local understandings of 'relevant content' (Bucher 2012a), while LinkedIn's system prioritizes 'people you know, talking about the things you care about' (Davies 2019). On the other hand, before becoming input data in a new set of computational iterations, the same field logics and culture are 'confounded' by the ubiquitous presence of algorithmic outputs – following the familiar pattern of the feedback loop, only on a much larger scale.

It is especially at this level – the level of the field, of the techno-social aggregate, counting hundreds of thousands of user–machine interactions every minute, or even every second – that important sociological questions about the *code in the culture* remain unanswered. Are the pre-digital field logics encapsulated by online platforms systematically *reinforced* by myriads of culturally aligned algorithmic interactions? Or, on the contrary, do the platform logics confounding online behaviour end up *transforming* the structure and *doxa* of the social fields they are applied to?

Both hypotheses have been explored theoretically in the existing critical literature, with some scholars stressing the technological *reinforcement* of an unequal social order (e.g. Benjamin 2019; Noble 2018; Eubanks 2018) and others pointing to the elements of *transformation* brought by the meshing of social and machine learning (e.g. Fourcade and Johns 2020; Cheney-Lippold 2017; Beer 2013a). Notably, these two techno-social processes are not mutually exclusive. Consider the case of online dating: the proliferation and widespread usage of dating apps and services might have reinforced socially constructed inequalities in 'erotic capital' (Hakim 2010). This is one likely effect of Tinder's 'desirability score', a measure computed to rank users and orchestrate their matches according to a simple, path-dependent model: 'if you are losing the Tinder game more often than not, you will likely never get to swipe on profiles clustered in the upper ranks' (Rolle 2019). However, the rise of Internet-mediated dating has also contributed to a limited yet unprecedented emancipation of romantic relations from the traditionally powerful social constraints of geography, religion, race and class homophily (Rosenfeld and Thomas 2012), thus driving a digital transformation of the 'sexual field' (Martin and George 2006).

The changeability of user–machine interactions, techno-logical infrastructures and algorithmic code across contexts as well as over time makes it hard to produce general conclusions on the techno-social mechanisms in play within platformized fields. Given this uncertainty, and in order to illustrate the field-level dynamics of the code in the culture, I will focus on an 'exemplary case in a finite world of possible configurations' (Bourdieu 2002: 268), namely, YouTube in the mid 2010s. Below I present empirical evidences of how automated video recommendations are likely to have at once *reinforced* and *transformed* the pre-digital cultural logics of fields of music consumption.

Reinforcing, or transforming?

More than just a video-sharing platform, YouTube is by far the most used music streaming service in the world (IFPI 2018), currently counting more than 2 billion users worldwide (YouTube 2020). My research work has focused on a very special social agent, in charge of the classification and circulation of the hundreds of hours of video content uploaded every second: the related videos algorithm.

This artificial social agent is one of YouTube's best-known computational features, widely indicated as the main source of video views on the platform (Wu, Rizoiu and Xie 2019; Celma 2010: 3). This recommender algorithm is programmed to show 'a ranked list of related videos' in response to the video that a user is currently viewing (Bendersky et al. 2014: 1). Between 2014 and 2015, I collected large amounts of data regarding the types of music content 'related' by the automated system, both internationally (Airoldi, Beraldo and Gandini 2016) and within the Italian musical field (Airoldi 2021).

The exact formulation of the algorithm is not publicly disclosed, but papers by Google researchers suggest that, at the time of my data collection, the system paired video content largely based on a collaborative filtering logic; that is, if many users watched video B right after video A, these two videos were likely to then be algorithmically 'related' (Bendersky et al. 2014; see Celma 2010). Socialized through data traces of global co-viewing patterns, this unsupervised machine learning system practically encapsulates the broad 'classificatory imagination' of musical fields (Beer 2013b), adapting in real time to their continuous fluctuations. Just as music lovers know that Dizzy Gillespie's recordings are closely related to Charlie Parker's – in terms of genre,

production context and mutual collaborations – and, simultaneously, very distant from Finnish metal, this socialized
machine does so too, in a purely practical way. The joint
consumption of music videos about bebop jazz and Finnish
metal is a too rare practice for the algorithm to present
these items as related. On the contrary, since Gillespie and
Parker videos are frequently uploaded by the same YouTube
channels and featured in the same bebop playlists, they
are likely to be co-viewed and, as a result, to be automatically paired by the machine – to assist or, eventually, nudge
music publics. You might recognize a feedback loop here:
automated video recommendations are computed based on
platform users' viewing patterns; the same viewing patterns
are massively confounded by the presence of automated
video recommendations; once again, these become input data
in a new iteration – and so on.

In recent years, sociologists studying music consumption
have become increasingly aware of the fact that – to borrow
Beer's words – 'algorithms are also drawing cultural boundaries and influencing where these boundaries are placed and
where divisions occur' (2013a: 97). Still, the extent to which
the boundaries characterizing the field of music consumption
have been *reinforced* or *transformed* by the activities of
platform-based machines has so far been a widely theorized
but empirically understudied topic (Beer 2013b; Barile and
Sugiyama 2015; Webster 2019). Aiming to explore the field-
level effects of YouTube's recommender system on music
classification, Davide Beraldo, Alessandro Gandini and I
analysed a sample of 22,141 related music videos, mapping
networks of algorithmic associations among heterogeneous
music content on the platform. Our study showed how
clusters of frequently related videos – essentially, filter bubbles
of recommended content – clearly overlapped specific music
genres, such as 1990s rock, teen pop, Irish music, Arabic
pop, gangsta rap, polka, trap music, K-pop, Ugandan music,
etc. (Airoldi, Beraldo and Gandini 2016).

This preliminary finding suggests that the YouTube recommender system was actually *reinforcing* the pre-digital genre
logics of the musical field. However, our network analysis
also identified bubbles of related music that deviated from
conventional classifications. That is, clusters of recommended

videos featuring relaxing natural sounds, hairdryer noises, bedtime lullabies for babies, background music for sleeping or meditation. These were related by the YouTube algorithm based on what we labelled in the paper a 'situational logic' of music reception, according to which the duration and contextual function of the consumed music matter more than its subcultural or artistic value. Such a situational logic has been traditionally regarded as a taboo within artistic fields, long-dominated by an anti-functional, Kantian, high-art style of aesthetic appreciation (Bourdieu 1983, 1984, 1993). Thus, the fact that the recommender system put forward this alternative aesthetic perspective signalled an ongoing, computationally induced *transformation* of musical fields and reception practices.

I have subsequently replicated this study on a different sample, composed of 14,865 related music videos uploaded by Italian YouTube accounts only (Airoldi 2021). This digitally encapsulated national field, dominated by domestic music, has allowed me to observe techno-social dynamics more closely.

A network visualization of the 14,865 videos related by the platform algorithm is presented on the left-hand side of Figure 4. Shades of grey indicate content of different music

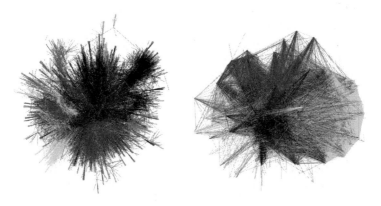

Figure 4 On the left-hand side, related music videos network (directed); on the right-hand side, commenter videos network (undirected). Shades of grey indicate music genres. Layouts: Yifan Hu and OpenOrd (Gephi). Based on Airoldi 2021.

categories. It is evident, even at first sight, how related videos form 'genre bubbles': in 90.3 per cent of the cases, the algorithmic system recommended videos of the same genre – a pattern particularly marked for Italian hip hop videos. Overall, the study portrays a general reinforcement of the pre-digital cultural boundaries segmenting the Italian musical field, encapsulated and amplified by the techno-social context of YouTube.

While the important role of related videos in driving user engagement on the platform is well known, the mere presence of cultural regularities in the documented algorithmic relations is not a sufficient condition to postulate their impact on listeners' consumption practices. In order to estimate the social effects of automated recommendations, I measured how users collectively interacted with recommended videos, based on data from 399,292 YouTube comments. My idea was that, if platform publics tend not to cross genre boundaries reinforced by the recommender system, forms of algorithmic confounding are likely to be in place and have behavioural consequences. The network analysis convincingly supported this hypothesis, showing that only a minority of YouTube commenters interacted with videos of multiple genres, despite the omnivorous attitude of contemporary music audiences (see Airoldi 2021). On the right side of Figure 4, the spatial distribution of shades in the network evidences how user–video interactions cluster along genre boundaries. Notably, Italian hip hop listeners are especially subjected to this genre-based confinement (cluster in light grey), perhaps as a result of the particularly homogeneous bubble of recommended content they were exposed to.

In sum, these empirical investigations provide some preliminary evidence of how YouTube's recommendation system picked up the 'classificatory imagination' (Beer 2013b) of music publics and reinforced socially recognized categorical boundaries by authoritatively shaping the circulation of content. Except for a few signs of a transformative 'situational' logic (Airoldi, Beraldo and Gandini 2016), relations among videos were culturally aligned with the *doxa* of the analysed musical fields. Beyond the specific case of music, Roth and colleagues have recently obtained comparable results from analysing related YouTube videos across broader categories, demonstrating that automated recommendations are 'often prone to confinement dynamics' (Roth, Mazières and Menezes 2020: 14). Hence, rather than expanding the diversity of content viewed by each user, related videos seem to lead to topical rabbit holes (Tufekci 2018), reinforcing the structure and boundaries of consumption fields.

Still, the case sketched above offers only a partial picture of the complex techno-social dynamics encapsulated and engineered by YouTube. In fact, personalized video recommendations based on users' local data contexts populate the homepage, and may alter how related videos are presented to single viewers (Covington, Adams and Sargin 2016; Roth, Mazières and Menezes 2020). Several other artificial agents swiftly modulate the visibility of content based on obscure and highly variable cultural criteria, such as the algorithms ranking YouTube search results (Rieder, Matamoros-Fernandez and Coromina 2018). On top of that, users often stream content through multiple platforms, thus diluting the behavioural reinforcement or transformation induced by one specific algorithmic system, as well as its cumulative effects on a field (Bruns 2019). Moreover, we must not forget the social ties keeping fields together. Interpersonal communication, enhanced and accelerated by platform connectivity, drives the boundary works and symbolic struggles underlying social change and cultural reproduction, in combination with the more-than-human relations of artificial social agents.

The epistemological complications of our techno-social world should not dissuade us from sociologically researching the code in the culture (Kitchin 2017). In some ways, we have no choice. Whether it is the case of political filter bubbles on Facebook (Hargreaves et al. 2018), stereotypical search results on Google (Noble 2018), or Tinder-powered romantic intercourses (Rolle 2019), it is more and more evident how machine learning systems have become intertwined with the fields of social life. The symbolic oppositions and social overlaps presented in the iconic two-dimensional diagrams of Bourdieu's *Distinction* (1984), statistically reconstructing the lifestyles of the French population within consumption fields, are now mediated not solely by the 'social unconscious' (Bourdieu 1981: 310) of class habitus but, increasingly, by a 'technological unconscious' (Beer 2009) – to the point that

behind every multiple correspondence analysis diagram
depicting taste clusterings [...] there could be algorithmic
processes lurking in the shadows, shaping those clusters
by influencing cultural knowledge, tastes and preferences.
Perhaps this is not just about cultural know-how and social
capital, perhaps it is something much more material that
is now a structural part of how culture is encountered,
consumed and disseminated. (Beer 2013a: 97)

However, there is good news for social scientists which has
passed quite unnoticed: the 'missing masses' (Latour 1992)
lurking in the shadows of the social are not that different
from us. The code is in the culture, but the culture – our
culture – is in the code. Socialized machines participate in
platformized fields by confounding them, but they largely
operate according to cultural logics absorbed from those
very same fields. This is what the aforementioned research
on YouTube recommendations ultimately suggests. It is also
what Noble (2018) tells us, by dissecting how the historical,
economic and institutional processes behind the systematic
discrimination of African Americans in the United States
have come to permeate search engines and their machine
learning systems, filled with indexed prejudices and predatory
ads imbued with the structural racism of a divided country
(Benjamin 2019), to be then reinforced by the 'degenerate
feedback loops' (Jiang et al. 2019) of the code in the culture.
     If Chapters 2 and 3 have served essentially to build
definitions, enumerate examples and disseminate doubts, the
following chapter will be dedicated to the systematization
and theorization of what has been said so far. The culture in
the code and the code in the culture are, after all, two sides
of the same coin. What ties them together is the machine
habitus.

4

A Theory of Machine Habitus

Premises

A simple exercise of 'sociological imagination' (Mills 1959):
imagine a new-born baby – a human being this time, in
flesh and blood. For the sake of this chapter, we will call
this fictitious character Andrea, and use an impersonal
pronoun, to remain vague about 'its' gender. Even from
within the mom's belly, Andrea could feel that society was
somehow out there. It could hear the music and voices in
the room, experience the organic food eaten by its mother,
or the vibrations of public transportation while she was on
her way to work. Then, once born, Andrea is catapulted
into a noisy and vastly unequal social world, eager to learn
and explore. As we have seen in Chapter 2, Andrea will
go through a *primary socialization* largely mediated by
the family environment, and then a number of *secondary
socialization* processes, linked to the various social fields
and groups one may encounter while growing up – such as
school friends, sport teammates, music fandoms, partners,
work colleagues, and more (Berger and Luckmann 1966).
The black-boxed outcome of all this is a *habitus*, that is,
a set of durable cultural dispositions produced by socially
structured conditions of existence (Bourdieu 1977). These
dispositions are crystallized in Andrea's brain as categories

of perception that, when confronted with sensorial inputs coming from the world out there, automatically generate action in response (Lizardo 2004). Hence, due to very different experiences and embodied histories (Bourdieu 1990a), a male, white and upper-class Andrea will see the world through a different *practical reason* compared to a female, black and working-class Andrea. Immersed in the same situation, these two imaginary Andreas will *likely* react differently (Lizardo 2013), and their distinct reactions will somehow contribute to the reproduction of the social world (Bourdieu and Wacquant 1992). For its part, the social world will likely give a quite different welcome to the two Andreas – at school (Bourdieu and Passeron 1990), in the workplace (Bourdieu 2001), on the streets (Wacquant 2002) – since their respective habitus-driven and socially situated practices are also classified and valued based on the *doxa* of structurally unequal and hierarchized fields.

Now, if we argue – as I have done in the previous chapters – that machine learning systems are also socialized, via the computational experience of human-generated data contexts, and thus similarly acquire durable cultural propensities working as a machine habitus, which are then actualized and recursively updated during human–machine interactions, a number of theoretical points remain to be addressed.

First, *in what ways do the processes of structural conditioning shaping the formation and practice of machine habitus diverge from what was originally theorized by Bourdieu for human subjects?* Or, put simply: to what extent can we push the metaphor of the machine habitus and see the behaviour of a socialized spam filter or social media bot as marked by privileges and social inequalities, as in the case of our Andrea? In the following section, I will discuss how social (and digital) *structures* impact all social agents, arguing that the structural grounds encapsulated by techno-social fields constrain and enable the social learning and actions of both humans and socialized machines.

Second, *how do cultural dispositions embodied as habitus and encoded as machine habitus practically mediate human–machine interactions within techno-social fields?* For instance, in what ways may automated music recommendations differ between a working-class Andrea and its upper-class alter ego? I will build on the typology of user–machine interactions drawn in Chapter 3 to theorize the dispositional mediation of techno-social *entanglements*.

Third, *how do techno-social feedback loops affect the distinct dispositional trajectories of humans and socialized machines, over time and across fields?* Put differently, how can Andrea's repeated interactions with a recommender system end up reshaping the cultural dispositions of both interacting agents? Also, what happens when a multiplicity of techno-social feedback loops and fields are simultaneously involved – e.g. as when Andrea relies on different platforms to stay informed? These questions are discussed in one section dedicated to the entangled *trajectories* of habitus and machine habitus.

Finally, *what could the aggregate effects of human–machine entanglements on techno-social fields be?* Imagine Andrea and millions of other users repeatedly interacting with the machine learning systems at work in platforms like Netflix, Facebook, Google Search or Instagram: can these myriad techno-social feedback loops contribute to shifting social regularities in cultural taste, consumption, spoken language or sociality? In the concluding section of the present chapter, I will speculate on how the machine habitus may contribute to a renegotiation of the powerful cultural *boundaries* that invisibly structure society while making it meaningful.

In sum, this chapter has the ambitious aim of reassembling the culture in the code and the code in the culture by outlining a theory of machine habitus in action, illuminating at once how society underlies the dynamic, platform-based interplay between machine learning systems and human users, and how it is broadly (re)produced as a result of this. While making extensive use of Bourdieu's classic concepts and ideas, here I also dare to stretch them in ways and directions intended to be useful to the sociological interpretation of contemporary societies and their fragmented more-than-human landscape (Lupton 2020). Theories are generalizations, and the present one is certainly no exception. This implies that my broad considerations about a highly unstable, opaque and complex matter such as the algorithmic systems populating digital platforms might risk producing oversimplifications. Using practical examples featuring Andrea as the main character, I will try to situate my abstract notions as much as possible in plausible real-life contexts.

One of the beautiful 'precepts' from the conclusion to Mills' *The Sociological Imagination* reads: 'try to understand men and women as historical and social actors, and the ways in which the variety of men and women are intricately selected and intricately formed by the variety of human societies' (Mills 1959: 225). Arguably, my proposal to understand machine learning systems as social agents intricately embedded within and shaped by platformized fields may raise some eyebrows. Seeing the very 'narrow' and hardly 'intelligent' (Broussard 2018) learning algorithms we ordinarily encounter online as participating in society in ways comparable to human subjects might appear as just another postmodern exaggeration. Still, as Chapter 2 illustrated, how a basic spam filter practically absorbs cultural propensities inscribed in past data patterns in order to formulate predictions is not too dissimilar from what more advanced and celebrated AI models do (Askell 2020; Kelleher 2019; Leviathan and Matias 2018; Silver and Hassabis 2017). Powerful machines like GPT-3, Google Duplex or AlphaGo can autonomously write essays, make phone calls and learn board games: it is certainly easier to understand *them* as somehow closer to us, their sentient biological counterparts. However, it is not the bare intelligence of a machine that makes it a social agent (Esposito 2017), nor the intelligibility of its final outputs for human subjects. What truly matters is whether the machine can learn from traces of the social world, and turn them into propensities to subsequently 'make a difference' within that world (Giddens 1984: 14). This is something both the GPT-3 and a banal spam filter do. It is also what any human subject does, by means of the habitus (see Bourdieu 1977).

Through the theoretical lens of the machine habitus, something otherwise difficult to notice becomes slightly clearer: although machine learning systems have no consciousness or meaningful understanding of reality, they contribute practically to the reproduction of society, with its arbitrary discourses, invisible boundaries, and structures.

Structures

Social structure
Machine habitus can be defined as the *set of cultural dispositions and propensities encoded in a machine learning system
through data-driven socialization processes.* Since such
dispositions and propensities derive from patterns in human-
generated data, they reflect social and cultural regularities
crystallized in the machine-readable data contexts used for
training and feedback (see Chapter 2). Therefore, similar to
a Bourdieusian social actor, a socialized machine 'wittingly
or unwittingly, willy nilly, is a producer and reproducer
of objective meaning', its actions being the product of a
modus operandi of which it 'is not the producer and has no
conscious mastery' (Bourdieu 1977: 79). The present section
examines to what extent the analogy between human subjects
and machine learning systems holds when we consider the
structural conditioning of action within techno-social fields.

According to Bourdieu, 'it is only in the relation to
certain structures that habitus produces given discourses
or practices' (Bourdieu and Wacquant 1992: 135). These
are the 'objective' social and symbolic divisions segmenting
fields, subjectively interiorized through socialization in the
form of habitus: 'There exists a correspondence between
social structures and mental structures, between objective
divisions in the social world – particularly into dominant
and dominated in the various fields – and the principles
of vision and division that agents apply to it' (Bourdieu
1989a: 7). On the one side, social structures are *external* to
social agents, crystallized in the material inequalities, norms,
institutions and *doxa* characterizing the fields these agents
are confronted with. For Bourdieu, any field can be seen as
constituted by a 'social space' understandable in geographical
terms, as divided into different regions corresponding to
various social classes (1989a: 16). The social space is an
abstract system of relations among positions in the structure,
characterized by different volumes of economic, cultural and
social capital (Bourdieu 1986), jointly working as 'symbolic
power' (Bourdieu 1989a). Spatial distances are equivalent to
social distances, separating distinct conditions of existence.

This topological metaphor can be stretched even further, by imagining a field's social space as a vast land that, in the proximity of disadvantaged social positions lacking all types of capital, becomes impervious and nearly uninhabitable. On the other side, the same social structures lie *inside* social agents. Objective positions in a field are internalized through socializing experiences and, by means of the mediation of the habitus, probabilistically generate regularities in the lifestyles, life goals and 'position-takings' of individuals close in social space (Bourdieu 1984, 2002).

Take the educational field as an example: the habitus of a young Andrea growing up in a poor Parisian *banlieue* is likely to be at odds with the French educational system. School programs and codified classroom relations reflect sedimented ideas of legitimacy – of knowledge, values, people and manners – which, according to Bourdieu (1966; Bourdieu and Passeron 1990), tacitly favour dominant social classes by 'reproducing' structural inequalities through forms of 'symbolic violence'. This does not mean that kids like Andrea are destined not to succeed at all in the 'game' of French education. However, if that happens, it will be in spite of the invisibilized symbolic and social barriers lying outside as well as inside the habitus, barriers that make the game significantly harder for Andrea than for the ideal, middle-class student already *habituated* to it.

Habitus is at once a 'structuring structure' and a 'struc-tured structure' (Bourdieu 1984: 170). As Calhoun and colleagues put it: 'structures are "structuring" in the sense that they guide and constrain action. But they are also "struc-tured" in the sense that they are generated and reproduced by actors' (2002: 260). This clearly recalls the recursive process through which the machine habitus contributes to the repro-duction of society. In fact, machine learning systems see and order the social world according to classificatory schemes which, far from being natural or neutral, are the cultural products of the practices, social struggles and logics of the techno-social fields they are immersed in. For instance, the social patterning of aesthetic preferences opposing middle-class and working-class, black and white, male and female music listeners, is ordinarily picked up by recommendation systems (Prey 2018), which pre-consciously actualize cultural propensities reflecting the users/trainers' positions in the social space, and likely reinforce them through music recommendations (Airoldi 2021).

Thus, once encoded in the form of data patterns, social structures do 'compress' the agency of socialized machines too (Boudon and Bourricaud 2003). However, since 'computational agency' (Tufekci 2015) is the lifeless result of a conscienceless practical reason (see Chapter 3), an obvious yet fundamental difference between the social conditioning of individual subjects and that of socialized machines exists: since they are not sentient subjects, machine learning systems do not suffer from – nor do they understand – the *external* constraints of social structures, such as poverty, physical and symbolic violence, or discrimination. While traces of the social order are certainly inscribed *inside* the machine habitus, artificial agents cannot but ignore the 'intimate dramas', 'deepest malaises' and 'most singular suffering' constellating symbolically dominated existences, which 'find their roots in the objective contradictions, constraints and double binds inscribed in the structures of the labor and housing markets, in the merciless sanctions of the school system, or in mechanisms of economic and social inheritance' (Bourdieu and Wacquant 1992: 201).

Digital infrastructure
Since the labour market and the school system Bourdieu wrote about are now encapsulated by LinkedIn and Coursera, and most fields of the social see some comparable form of platformization (Helmond 2015), it is important to consider another kind of structure too – that is, the digital infrastructures underlying techno-social fields.

The scholarly literature has similarly represented this second type of structure in topological and relational terms, as an 'environment', 'assemblage', 'network' or 'cyberspace' (see Plantin et al. 2018; Siles et al. 2020; Crawford and Joler 2018; Nunes 1997). As a structural layer additional to and intertwined with social structure, digital infrastructures are powerfully involved in the shaping of techno-social practice across information systems, platforms, apps and software more broadly (Plantin et al. 2018; Bucher and Helmond 2018; McKelvey 2018).

Again, the educational field is a case in point. During the Covid-19 emergency, education became all of a sudden dependent on computers, video-audio equipment, updated operating systems, stable Wi-Fi connections and competent users. Unsurprisingly, these material and cultural resources are unevenly distributed across schools and segments of the social space (Bacher-Hicks, Goodman and Mulhern 2021). A recent research report has shown how traditional social inequalities overlap digital inequalities among French school kids (Tricot and Chesné 2020). Hence, the unequal usage of information technologies risks adding further obstacles to the lives of disadvantaged students, while strengthening the privileges of those already attuned and committed to the 'conservative' cultural logics of the school system (Bourdieu 1966).

The possibility of having any agency at all within fields mediated by digital infrastructures depends on having access to those infrastructures in the first place. Individual participation in digital technologies and the Internet has significantly increased over the past decades, but a first-level digital divide still affects billions of people worldwide (Lutz 2019; IWS 2020). Inequalities in access to digital infrastructures concern machine learning systems too, since they can either be an integral part of techno-social fields – like the platform algorithms on Instagram (Cotter 2019) and Facebook (Bucher 2012b) – or struggle to gain and keep access, as with the millions of social bots clandestinely operating online, spreading disinformation while dodging content moderation (Bessi and Ferrara 2016).

For those lucky agents who do have access, further barriers imposed by software architectures nonetheless exist. In fact, whenever we use a mobile app, visit a website or play a videogame, we confront 'the digital walls and foundations that delimit our experience online' (Cheney-Lippold 2011: 166): the coded rules, navigational paths, configurations and procedures predetermined by designers and developers. These walls made of code produce the informational asymmetries structuring user–machine inter-actions in digital platforms (Chapter 3). Similar to a field's social space, a digital infrastructure can at once enable and constrain agency, while staying hidden in the background of social practice (Orlikowski 1992). Just as the physical properties of a mountain trail (its slope, or the solidity of the ground), along with its perceived difficulty on the part of a given trekker, 'afford' different styles of hiking, a given platform environment presents 'affordances' that both enable and constrain user experience (Bucher and Helmond 2018). Examples are Facebook's 'like' button, hashtags on Instagram, the 280-character limit on Twitter and, more generally, any sort of digital property prescribing for sociality, behaviour and communication (van Dijck 2013; Baym and boyd 2012). These platform features are mostly aimed at driving engagement, profitability and data mining (Zuboff 2019). Their capacity to do so effectively is likely to be inversely correlated with levels of digital literacy on the part of the users (Hargittai and Micheli 2019; Lutz 2019).

Hence, the affordances of digital environments, together with agents' more or less impervious locations in the social space, modulate possibilities of action. These two kinds of structure are, in practice, tightly intertwined: as we have seen, technologies are social products reflecting inequalities and cultural boundaries, which end up technologically shaping and confounding them in turn (MacKenzie and Wajcman 1999). Furthermore, it is important to note that agents' positions in the two structural layers are likely to overlap, since being able to access and expertly master information technologies is in effect a 'digital capital' (Ragnedda and Ruiu 2020; Calderón Gómez 2020; Levina and Arriaga 2014). Within techno-social fields, this form of capital is directly converted into platform-specific cultural capital, social capital and prestige (i.e. symbolic capital) – objectified by metrics such as the number of followers, video views, retweets or likes (Fourcade and Johns 2020; Arvidsson et al. 2016). In the case of digital influencers and their online 'visibility game', this conversion potentially extends beyond platform-specific capitals – notably, to economic capital – and works both ways (Cotter 2019).

Arguably, human agents are not the only ones whose agency is simultaneously conditioned by social structures and digital infrastructures. In order to formulate predictions and draw algorithmic distinctions, 'data hungry' (Fourcade and Johns 2020) machine learning systems seek informational capital – which, like the other capitals theorized by Bourdieu, consists of accumulated (digital) labour (1986: 241). Bots ferociously fight over edits in the back end of Wikipedia's infrastructure (Tsvetkova et al. 2017; Geiger 2017). Trading algorithms queue to place their financial orders, and the matching engines that organize these queues must do so in accordance with stock market regulations (D. MacKenzie 2019). The very same reCAPTCHA system that on the one side obliges an unwitting human user to annotate training data in order to access a website, is designed to deny access to a malicious AI software on the other (Mühlhoff 2020).

Hence, by participating in techno-social fields along with human users, machine learning systems also have to cope with structural constraints of both digital and social kinds. Even though socialized machines will probably never be 'in our world' (Fjelland 2020: 8), our world already lies within them, in the form of socially structured dispositions deployed on digital infrastructures. Below, I discuss what this means for the sociological understanding of human–machine interactions.

Entanglements

Having examined the structural foundations of human and computational agency, I now concentrate on the connections between the two: that is, the *entanglements* of practice that tie individual habitus and machine habitus together.

The techno-social character of everyday life emphasized throughout this book will hardly sound new to readers familiar with STS and ANT literature. More than a decade ago, organization scholar Wanda Orlikowski wrote about the 'recursive intertwining of humans and technology in practice' in the following, relevant terms:

> the architecture of the Google search engine involves multiple servers, directories, databases, indexes, and algorithms, and reflects considerable choices made about its design, construction, and operation [...]. As Google crawls and indexes the web constantly, the PageRank algorithm is continually updating its ranking of web pages because the underlying

link structure of the web is changing all the time. Not only
are web pages being added to and deleted from the web every
day, but existing web pages are being modified, with links
added and deleted. And these ongoing changes are reflected
in the PageRank algorithm's ongoing updating of Google
indexes [...]. The Google search engine is computer code that
was produced and is maintained by software engineers, that
executes on computers (configured with particular hardware
and software elements), and whose operation depends on
the millions of people who create and update web pages
everyday, and the millions of people who enter particular
search terms into it. The result is a constitutive entanglement
of the social and the material. (Orlikowski 2007: 1439–40)

Orlikowski (1992), along with several other scholars
(e.g. Latour and Woolgar 1986; Knorr Cetina 2009;
D. MacKenzie 2019), has researched socio-material entanglements especially at the level of organizations and situated
interactions. However, as 'interpersonal relations are never,
except in appearance, individual-to-individual relationships'
(Bourdieu 1977: 81), so the entanglements between humans
and machine learning systems have cultural ramifications that
lie deep below the interactional surface (Sterne 2003). The
above account of the multiple techno-social entanglements
characterizing Google Search, while rightly focusing on the
long-neglected materiality and dynamism of social practice,
tends to leave the 'context of context' out of the picture
(Askegaard and Linnet 2011) – that is, culture, history, social
structure. The theory of machine habitus aims to bring this
socio-cultural matter back in the study of human–machine
interactions.

Let me illustrate this point with an example. What if a
female, non-white version of our Andrea searches for 'black
girls' on a search engine and, to her surprise, the machine
learning system returns a page filled with porn? – as really
happened to Safiya Umoja Noble, the author of *Algorithms
of Oppression* (2018: 18). The propensities practically transforming Andrea's prompt 'black girls' into this specific
output largely derive from the continuous inductive analysis
of patterns in global data contexts, detected based on the
specific prescriptions of the system's *deus in machina*. As
Noble painstakingly shows, search engines' global data

contexts are marked by the racist, sexist and predatory culture dominant in white straight male America, and thus hardly reflect Andrea's dominated position in the social space. Yet, via machine socialization, socially located cultural views get encoded as machine habitus, are reproduced during human–machine interaction, and may then eventually be realigned by Andrea's 'local' feedback – e.g. ignoring search results, or reporting the issue.

First, this example shows how the entanglements of socialized machines and their users are mediated at once by digital infrastructures and social structures. It is not just two ontologically distinct agents interacting through the platform interface: together with them, there are embodied histories and encoded cultural propensities – habitus and machine habitus.

Furthermore, the same example allows me to reiterate why the machine habitus should not be seen as a mere reflex of individual habitus. In fact, the specific instantiation of the search algorithm – which, for the sake of the present theory, we consider as a single social agent (see Chapter 2) – and the female, non-white Andrea base their practical reasoning on different sets of dispositions. As we saw in Chapter 3, these can be weakly or strongly aligned, so producing different interactional outcomes, in combination with the affordances of a digital infrastructure – such as its degree of informational asymmetry. This also implies that a different user searching 'black girls' – for instance, a white supremacist man, with a radically distinct worldview and habitus – would be less shocked and upset than Andrea if faced with the same racist and sexist content.

The situated entanglement between a socialized machine and its users 'owes its form to the objective structures which have produced the dispositions of the interacting agents' (Bourdieu 1977: 81). Depending on their socialization, agents will see the world, behave and interact differently. In the case of supervised machine learning systems, the solidification of socially structured dispositions passes first through the global data contexts of preliminary training data, then through a 'local' fine-tuning stage. For unsupervised machine learning algorithms, such as those frequently employed in search engines or on social media, it is common that global and local data contexts are both involved in secondary machine socialization (see Chapter 2).

When artificial and human agents have incorporated 'the same history' (Bourdieu 1990a: 58), a sense of taken-for-grantedness and 'immediate adherence' characterizes the entanglement. This happens, for instance, when culturally aligned music recommendations smoothly suit a consumer's mood and taste. A usual way of interpreting such an interactional configuration would imply making use of the popular jargon of marketing: the recommender algorithm correctly understands 'intimate desires', and fulfils 'individual needs' by offering 'personalised experiences' in order to increase 'customer satisfaction' (Darmody and Zwick 2020). However, by now it should be clear that there is 'nothing personal' in automated music recommendations (Prey 2018), nor in consumers' tastes (Bourdieu 1984). In both cases, there is only an illusion of personalization, subjectivity and uniqueness. On the one hand, machine learning systems see each user as a set of data points more or less correlated to other 'dividual' data points (see Cheney-Lippold 2017; Prey 2018; A. Mackenzie 2018) – a process comparable to how social categorization works among humans, except for the mathematics involved. On the other hand, users' tastes, far from being subjective, are the naturalized product of shared social conditions, regulated by tacit cultural hierarchies and classifications (Bourdieu 1984). As a result, individuals occupying similar positions in the social world will share similar ways of appreciating, classifying and judging aesthetic products – in virtue of a similar socialization, marked by similar social experiences.

If the power of the habitus' 'social unconscious' (Bourdieu 1981: 310) lies in its invisibility, resulting from the ideological reduction of individual practice to purely subjective will, interests, rationality or talent (Bourdieu and Wacquant 1992; Bourdieu 1984), the power of algorithms and AI similarly lies in the ideological removal of the social from the computational black box – which is therefore narrated as neutral, objective or super-humanly accurate (Broussard 2018; Beer 2017; Natale and Ballatore 2020; Campolo and Crawford 2020). Ideologies notwithstanding, in the background of any user–machine interaction lies a deeper entanglement, linking human and artificial agents to a field's *doxa* and social positions, by means of habitus and machine habitus. It is especially in virtue of a common cultural ground of machine-readable data and stored propensities that a recommender system can become attuned with the sedimented experiences of a music listener – for example, by proposing Britpop tracks to a nostalgic European millennial. And it is the algorithmic misrecognition of socially rooted user expectations that produces misaligned entanglements, leading to computational nudges, or overt misunderstandings (see Chapter 3).

The collective character of the experiential ground producing individual dispositions is a defining dimension of the very notion of habitus – even prior its development by Bourdieu, in the earlier connotations given to it by Marcel Mauss and Norbert Elias (Sterne 2003; Lizardo 2013). The habitus is at once subjective and objective: on the one side, an individual habitus; on the other, a class, gender or professional habitus, fabricating social regularities (Bourdieu 1984, 2001; Bourdieu and Wacquant 1992). With the massive implementation of machine learning systems, the cultural dispositions constituting the habitus of specific social groups and classes have penetrated, through proxy variables and data patterns, the statistically inductive models these social groups and classes are digitally entangled with.

Of course, the novelty of my thesis can be debated. After all, 'the nonhumans take over the selective attitudes of those who engineered them' (Latour 1992: 158; see also Akrich 1992). Cultural assumptions are crystallized by design in any technology, whether intelligent or not, in the form of a *deus in machina*. And, when technologies become 'embodied in lived practice', they always contribute to shaping the collective habitus and social fields where they are deployed (Sterne 2003: 385). Nonetheless, what is truly peculiar to the age of machine learning is *how* the social has become entangled with the technical and the material – that is, through dynamic, ubiquitous cultural learning processes comparable to human socialization (Fourcade and Johns 2020) – and the scale at which this has happened.

Billions of socialized machines and billions of users/trainers interact through feedback loops mediated, at once, by digital infrastructures and social structures. From being a static architecture, algorithmic code has turned into an adaptive, generative mechanism involved in an active relationship with the social environment (Cheney-Lippold 2011; Kelleher 2019; Rahwan et al. 2019; Pasquinelli 2017). This implies that relational shifts in stimuli at the level of a techno-social field – such as a new trending hashtag on Twitter, or an emerging purchasing pattern on Amazon – are likely to reverberate with both machine habitus and users' habitus; and, even more interestingly, that a change in users' inclinations is likely to resonate with the entangled machines' inclinations displayed in a new iteration, and vice versa. Therefore, a slight curiosity about the British royal family, witnessed by search or streaming data, will eventually produce an adjustment in the content recommended on Netflix. Then, since 'it is likely that the films that are recommended to you by these algorithmic processes are likely to become the films you watch or that you are likely to want to watch' (Beer 2013a: 81), a corresponding adjustment may take place on the user side.

The feedback loops between socialized machine learning systems and their entangled users/trainers can assume multiple, mutable configurations, with a range of possible interactional and field-level outcomes. This variability is partly due to the fact that the practical reason resulting from the machine habitus works in probabilistic terms: outputs are not modelled a priori, deterministically, as in rule-following systems guided solely by developers' *deus in machina*. Rather, they emerge inductively, as 'regulated improvisations', produced by 'adjusting to the demands inscribed as objective potentialities in the situation' (Bourdieu 1977: 78) – or, put differently, through the practical encounter between socially structured propensities and flows of input data. The feedback-based sedimentation of such correlational experiences can produce a stabilization or an adjustment of the encoded propensities, making the artificial agent gradually evolve, if it is programmed to do so – yet without entirely erasing the bulk of primary dispositions. At the opposite end of platform interfaces, humans are exposed, knowingly or not, to tailored algorithmic outputs, perceived through cultural lenses absorbed during socialization and embodied early on as habitus. If such exposure is repeated for long enough, users' habitual practices and cultural inclinations might be reinforced or transformed as well, along the lines of actions drawn by the computational authority.

Two fundamental aspects of user–machine entanglements need further clarification. These are their temporality – that is, how they develop over time – and multiplicity – that is, the fact that they are simultaneously linked to multiple socio-material grounds. Below I discuss how both temporality and multiplicity shape the entangled dispositional *trajectories* of agents within techno-social fields.

Trajectories

Temporality
Feedback loops are usually represented as circles, given their recursive character. A circle line ends where it begins, but this is not the case with user–machine interactions. In fact, every iteration of the feedback loop slightly changes the system and its agents, by producing either a reinforcement of pre-existing inclinations or their gradual transformation. If we take temporality into account, a user–machine entanglement can be portrayed as a spiral: the longer it revolves, the more it changes, moving away from its origin (Amoore 2019: 11). During the interactional process of reciprocal adjustment characterizing entanglements, the dispositional ground shared by two agents, as well as the cultural distance between them, inevitably change, affecting the diachronic trajectory of techno-social practice.

In the previous chapter, I argued that habitus and machine habitus are both path-dependent mechanisms. In machine learning systems, path-dependence is a statistical consequence of the data examples through which a model has been trained and the machine habitus' dispositions formed. For a neural network whose goal is to recognize images of fruit, an apple is such only if the vectorized set of values associated to the label 'apple' in the training data probabilistically resembles the set of values observed in a previously unseen picture. Therefore, a deep learning model socialized through a dataset featuring only red apples will struggle to recognize green apples, and a considerable amount of human feedback will be needed in order to correct *ex post* the encoded bias. Here you can think of other, comparable examples, such as a recommender system trying to estimate which products customers will be 'also interested in' based on past purchasing patterns, or a credit scoring model that predicts which loans are likely to default based on individual credit histories. Despite researchers and developers' active efforts to reduce path-dependent data biases, in general 'the more data that has been ingested by a machine learning system, the less revolutionary, reconfigurative force might be borne by any adventitious datum that it encounters' (Fourcade and Johns 2020).

Individual habitus is path-dependent for the very same reason: the sedimentation of past experiences as cultural schemas and dispositions, and their perceptual and classificatory influence on present and future practices. For example, if you grow up in a big house, then you will be more likely to feel at home in a big house rather than a small apartment. Notably, the outcome is not predetermined, but only likely. As Lizardo put it:

> Because the habitus is the product of adaptation to conditions, it is heavily predisposed to attempt to re-create the very same conditions under which the systems of skills and dispositions that it has most proficiently acquired can be most profitably put to use. [...] In this respect, the habitus is heavily weighted toward the past and biases choices in a way that lead [*sic*] to the conservation and constant reinforcement of already acquired capacities. (Lizardo 2013: 406)

The habitus and machine habitus actualize cultural dispositions crystallized in the past and working in the present as an embodied history. Yet, in the meantime, the social world might have changed in a way that puts the old dispositions at odds with the new tacit rules and *doxa* of a field. When this happens, there is a mismatch between habitus and the cultural environment in which it is deployed – what Bourdieu calls a 'hysteresis effect' (Strand and Lizardo 2017). An example frequently mentioned by the sociologist is the cultural lag between the 'precapitalist habitus' of Algerian peasants and the capitalist environment imposed on them by French colonizers in the 1950s, resulting in the coexistence of two chronological horizons: the precolonial past and the colonized present (Bourdieu and Wacquant 1992: 130).

According to Strand and Lizardo, the notion of hysteresis helps us to understand the 'systematic production of matches and mismatches within the context of dynamically changing, asynchronous, agent–environment couplings that characterize action', by revealing the 'close connection between action and temporality' (2017: 170–1). This remains valid for the faster unfolding of techno-social feedback loops. Whenever an artificial agent's propensities are perceived to be 'out of sync' with respect to the encountered data contexts (Bucher 2017: 35), we observe the hysteresis of machine habitus.

As misaligned machines try to catch up by ingesting feedback data, misaligned humans tend to do the same. Picture Andrea as a PhD graduate who has recently been lucky enough to become assistant professor. For a while, she will likely carry the old graduate school dispositions in the performance of the new role. These will perhaps make her feel a bit like an imposter, at least for a time, before she finally gets accustomed to the 'rhythm' of professorial habits (Strand and Lizardo 2017: 176). Still, for Bourdieu, such a cultural realignment is not always possible. In his work, the dispositional traces of one's social origin are described as extremely persistent even in the case of an ascendant (or descendant) social mobility (Lizardo 2013) – as with *parvenues*, who 'presume to join the group of legitimate, i.e. hereditary, possessors of the legitimate manner, without being the product of the same social conditions' and, as a result,

> are trapped, whatever they do, in a choice between anxious hyper-identification and the negativity which admits its defeat in its very revolt: either the conformity of an 'assumed' behaviour whose very correctness or hyper-correctness betrays an imitation, or the ostentatious assertion of difference which is bound to appear as an admission of inability to identify. (Bourdieu 1984: 95)

Several scholars have rightly criticized Bourdieu for a latent structural determinism, implicit in the supposed unchangeability of individual habitus (e.g. King 2000; Jenkins 1993). Building on the post-Bourdieusian work of Bernard Lahire

(2004, 2019), I argue that ongoing forms of experiential learning and differential secondary socializations can bring, in the medium and long term, important adjustments to durably interiorized cultural dispositions – and, therefore, can partly reorient agents' trajectories within fields. In this view, the mismatch between Bourdieu's *parvenues* and their hierarchical cultural field is not necessarily permanent: it can represent a momentary phase – a sort of analogue version of the computational 'cold start problem' (Celma 2010), yet complicated by very human logics of social distinction and competition.

Once again, these considerations generally hold true also in the case of artificial agents and their machine habitus, but with an important difference: rather than depending solely on accretive learning paths, the time decay (or durability) of their encoded dispositions is established by parameters chosen and updated by machine creators (see Chapter 2). Such design decisions depend on the specific goals assigned to the algorithmic system. For instance, Facebook's algorithm values recent user feedback more than older interactions, aiming to fill the newsfeed with 'fresh' content (Bucher 2012a: 1167). Also, music recommendation models value simultaneously the 'familiarity' and 'novelty' of content, and thus are likely to work based on combinations of past user data and present global patterns (Celma 2010: 102). Needless to say, the variability of machine habitus' 'temporality by design' further complicates the synchronization of agents' cultural 'clocks'.

Overall, it can be argued that each of the human and artificial agents entangled within techno-social fields can potentially follow distinct temporalities, depending on their contingent alignment with a common cultural ground and ever-changing *doxa* – only to experience, from time to time, an 'immediate adherence', a match in their field trajectories (Bourdieu 1990a). Oscillating and revolving at different cultural rhythms, user–machine feedback loops unfold diachronically like a dance: at T1, related YouTube videos imperfectly mirror cultural boundaries in the musical field, based on accumulated data on users' viewing patterns at T0; at T2, platform users' viewing practices are mediated by aesthetic expectations resulting from previous musical experiences, including those with related videos at T1 – and so on. These entanglements draw spirals, by moving from transformative stages, when users lag behind, to moments of reinforcement, with machines amplifying social patterns. This way, 'Far from being the automatic product of a mechanical process, the reproduction of social order accomplishes itself only through the strategies and practices via which agents temporalize themselves and make the time of the world' (Bourdieu and Wacquant 1992: 139).

Multiplicity
In attempting to clarify how habitus and machine habitus evolve as a result of recursive human–machine interactions, I have so far considered two entangled social agents in isolation. However, a platform user can simultaneously interact with many machine learning systems, which can in turn bear dispositional traces acquired from different human subjects. This section deals with the implications of this 'multiplicity' on social agents' dispositional trajectories.

We have seen how, through a primary socialization, human and artificial agents acquire a general knowledge about the world. Children's early experiences in the family context are embodied as durable sets of transposable dispositions, culturally biased by the family's particular position in the social space. In a similar way, supervised machine learning systems, like the fruit-recognition neural network in the example above, absorb culturally biased propensities from the global data contexts of the training datasets selected for them by machine creators. Then, a secondary socialization leads to a specialization – a local tuning of the global dispositions crystallized during the primary socialization. For example, during this phase, a young PhD candidate like Andrea will gradually discover the backstage of academic research, or an intelligent spam filter will get to know the field-specific data context in which it is put to work, thus adapting its propensities to the distinct textual nuances of phishing emails targeted at academics (see Figure 3) – or at gardeners, bank account holders, expats, gamers, and so on.

Once a grown-up human and a trained spam filter finally become entangled in the socio-material environment of an online mailbox, their distinct dispositional universes sedimented as habitus and machine habitus meet and mutually adjust to each other, through the spiral dance of alignments and misalignments discussed above. However, here comes a major, aforementioned difference between an individual subject and an artificial agent: the first can have multiple email accounts, and be simultaneously an academic, a gardener, a bank account holder, an expat and a gamer, whereas the socialized spam filter is inexorably paired to one email account and one digital infrastructure.

Contrary to artificial agents, human agents have a multiplicity of interpersonal relations, social circles and socio-material entanglements, affecting the habitus in potentially contradictory ways. In other words, humans have a life, while algorithms can at best simulate one. In order to understand agents' practices and dispositional trajectories within techno-social fields, one cannot but take into account the synchronic variations of multiple user–machine entanglements.

Consider the following example. To stay informed, our female academic Andrea uses the 'For You' section of Google News, which presents recent news stories algorithmically selected based on past search queries and behavioural traces. On top of that, she gets constant updates from her social media contacts and favourite media outlets via Facebook, which are pre-filtered and ranked by the newsfeed algorithm based on propensities derived from Andrea's datafied platform practices. Apart from these user–machine interactions, Andrea's news consumption consists in browsing the homepage of a couple of online newspapers, and watching some television in the evening.

At a given moment in time, the Google News and Facebook algorithms might be both aligned with Andrea's tacit expectations in terms of news, and thus jointly reinforce her cultural dispositions. If this is the case, the substantial content presented by the two machine learning systems may vary significantly based on the contingent flow of public opinion, but the framing and style will likely remain constant: a bubble of liberal journalistic discourses attuned with the urban lifestyle of a young academic. However, there is also the concrete possibility of a mismatch between one of the two entangled machines and Andrea's habitus, which could thus weaken the liberal filter bubble. For instance, if one of Andrea's closest friends becomes a fervent Christian conservative, the hysteresis of the Facebook newsfeed will continue by inertia to prioritize this friend's posts for a while, although Andrea is ideologically and 'dispositionally' very far from that cultural universe. Depending on her reaction – whether providing explicit feedback to the machine, to hide this content; a disillusionment, eventually leading to her disconnection from the platform; or, conversely, an unanticipated curiosity on her part for this religious and political conversion – the outcome will be either a feedback-based algorithmic realignment or a nudge-based transformative trajectory on the part of the user. Meanwhile, untouched by all that, Google News' artificial agent will keep going with its original classificatory practices, thus reinforcing Andrea's original bubble.

A single artificial agent is usually one element in a multifaceted, multi-directed bundle of techno-social practice (Ananny 2016), generated by and perceived through more or less aligned dispositions, within more or less informationally asymmetric digital infrastructures. So far, theoretical accounts of the social power of algorithms have generally tended to downplay the multiple and often contradictory techno-social influences digital consumers are subjected to, across platforms, devices and fields (Bruns 2019; Neyland 2019). Concretely, a single political advertising campaign created ad hoc by Cambridge Analytica and distributed to micro-targeted Facebook profiles hardly has the power to magically shift the voting intentions of a citizen from day to night (Rokka and Airoldi 2018). Rather, it is a whole network of human and more-than-human relations, resonating with a coherent cultural ground, that may eventually produce a change in behaviour. Otherwise, the most likely user reaction to a misaligned output would be to provide an implicit or explicit feedback, slightly realigning the machine habitus in a new step of the algorithmic dance; more rarely, forms of disillusionment and resistance might arise (Ruckenstein and Granroth 2020; Velkova and Kaun 2019). The exceptions are those entanglements in which the machine is powerfully involved in determining the capitals at stake in the field – such as in the entanglement between Uber's algorithmic systems and computationally managed drivers (Rosenblat and Stark 2016). In these cases, users have a (socially defined) interest in consciously conforming to the machine's nudges and predictions (Cotter 2019).

Since Andrea, like any one of us, is entangled with a considerable number of socialized machines across techno-social fields – Google News, Facebook, Twitter, Spotify, ResearchGate, YouTube, Netflix, Alexa, the email app, the bank app, the health-tracking app – we might wonder whether this implies that these machine learning systems all somehow mirror the same individual habitus (Jacobsen 2020). After all, in Bourdieu's work, the habitus is described as a 'matrix of perceptions' which is both durable and 'transposable' (Bourdieu 1977: 95) – that is, analogically transferrable from field to field, thanks to 'homological' relations among them determined by social structures (Bourdieu 1983). Due to this transposability, the cross-platform practices of the same user should be somehow coherent in terms of their *modus operandi*. Still, according to Bernard Lahire (2004, 2019), in reality the individual habitus is less homogeneous and transposable than Bourdieu presupposed. Even the family universe, where the dispositional foundations of an individual are laid, is rarely a coherent emanation of just one social class, since 'the family is very often made up of different heritages, sometimes contrasted, between the spouses who rarely share the same social properties (social and cultural origin, social positions, educational level or type of diploma, etc.), and this is not without consequence from the point of view of the socialisation of children' (Lahire 2019: 5). Therefore, the artificial agents Andrea ordinarily interacts with will probably not reflect a coherent block of collectively shared dispositions, but rather scattered data fragments of a multifaceted practical reason, built from multiple primary and secondary socializing influences and life experiences. In theory, a certain dispositional coherence would be at least expectable within the context of one field – that of music consumption, for instance, simulta-neously encapsulated by Spotify and YouTube. However, also in this case, the machine habitus of the two platforms' recommender systems, albeit entangled and aligned with the same subject, will not perfectly overlap with each other, for a different reason that we shall not forget: the code. In fact, the two algorithmic codes work according to different computational methods and *dei in machina*, determining the decay of old propensities, as well as the role of local and global data contexts in predicting the recommendations (Prey 2018; Covington, Adams and Sargin 2016). While local data contexts reflect Andrea's own practices and dispositions, global data contexts bear the (aggregate) imprint of many other machine trainers' practices and dispositions (see Chapter 2). Since platform algorithms often make use of global and local feedback data in combination, a multiplicity of heterogeneous dispositional elements can coexist not only within the individual habitus, but in the machine habitus too – complicating, as a result, the diachronic unfolding of agents' trajectories and practices.

In sum, it is evident that this overall picture of user–machine entanglements within techno-social fields lacks the neat lines and clear-cut rules a reader could have eventually expected from a sociology of algorithms. After all, aren't algorithms just formalized procedures and computational recipes? Yes, but they are social agents too, moved by heterogeneous and always shifting dispositions, interacting in diachronically and synchronically contradictory directions. Rather than perfectly meeting or nudging their users' needs and wants – as, respectively, in the techno-optimistic myth of personalization and in the techno-pessimistic myth of manipulation – machine learning systems negotiate with them a common cultural ground, iteration after iteration, feedback after feedback. The sum of these non-linear trajectories ultimately brings about the techno-social reproduction of society. Is this a purely entropic process, or one that presents social regularities? To answer this question we must embrace techno-social fields as a whole, and look closely at their boundaries.

Boundaries

Social, symbolic and automated
In this concluding section, I speculate on how socialized machines can contribute to transforming or reinforcing the symbolic and social boundaries of techno-social fields, thus

adding some theoretical ground to the discussion proposed at the end of Chapter 3.

Michèle Lamont and Virag Molnár have brought the notion of 'boundary' to the very centre of the contemporary sociological debate. They define social boundaries as 'objectified forms of social differences manifested in unequal access to and unequal distribution of resources (material and nonmaterial) and social opportunities' (2002: 168). This first type of boundary corresponds to inequalities in the allocation of economic, social and cultural capital, segmenting the social space of Bourdieusian fields. In contrast, symbolic boundaries are 'conceptual distinctions made by social actors to categorize objects, people, practices, [...] tools by which individuals and groups struggle over and come to agree upon definitions of reality' (Lamont and Molnár 2002: 168). Within fields, this second type of boundary marks asymmetries in symbolic power manifested in the *doxa* – those taken-for-granted norms and discourses separating right from wrong, legitimate from illegitimate, fine from vulgar, beautiful from ugly (Bourdieu 1984, 1989a, 1990a).

At this point, a short recapitulation might be beneficial. We have seen how an artificial agent's machine habitus can be entangled with its user's habitus, and that the two agents' path-dependent practices and multiple dispositions mutually adjust over time, piloting the entanglement in non-linear directions. All this may seem quite abstract, but it is what ordinarily happens when we get lost in the rabbit hole of YouTube's related videos, or in the visual stream of the Instagram feed. The machine learning system leads the recursive dance by fulfilling the 'need to eliminate some of the choices' and 'ease users' decision' (Celma 2010: 4). We react by either skipping or watching the recommended video, or scrolling past or liking the next Instagram pic, thus providing feedback that reinforces or transforms the filtering dispositions of the machine habitus. Our skipping and scrolling criteria will also be reinforced or transformed after repeated sessions of automated suggestions – and so too the classificatory schemes of our habitus. The awareness of this techno-social dance will depend on the digital infrastructure's informational asymmetries, as well as on the user's digital skills.

One might object that slight changes in habits produced by narrow machine learning systems bear no particular importance. After all, weren't those computationally recommended videos and pictures already available on the platforms, uploaded by some human? Sure. Couldn't the user have simply typed in the search bar to find them? Unlikely. As a matter of fact, this objection forgets the practical logics of social life theorized by Bourdieu (1977, 1990a). In fact, the YouTube or Instagram user's space of possibility, online as well as anywhere else, is pre-filtered in advance by the habitus: 'the most improbable practices are excluded, either totally, without examination, as unthinkable, or at the cost of the double negation which inclines agents to make a virtue of necessity, that is, to refuse what is anyway refused and to love the inevitable' (Bourdieu 1977: 77). This explains why the mere fact that an art exhibition is free does not mean that a lower-educated citizen will consider the possibility of going to it as 'thinkable'. The same can be said of the free music concerts, movies and make-up tutorials available on platforms, whose consumption or non-consumption, as well as style of consumption – e.g. ironic or serious (Jarness 2015) – depends heavily on users' education, age and gender (Mihelj, Leguina and Downey 2019).

My main point here is that, within techno-social fields, two intertwined filtering mechanisms jointly contribute to the social construction of reality and its boundaries, by defining how we subjectively experience our world, and how the social world is objectively divided: habitus and machine habitus. Through their encoded sets of cultural dispositions, machine learning algorithms – 'the merely technical' – actively participate in the reproduction of 'the social' (Law 1990: 8) and its structural barriers.

As shown for the music recommendation and reception clusters on YouTube presented at the end of the previous chapter, the socio-cultural roots of these entangled classificatory mechanisms generate observable regularities, which draw invisible boundaries confining similar social positions and 'position-takings' – constituting the relational spaces of a field (Bourdieu 2002). Such boundary processes are not a digital novelty: people's social networks have always been segregated by forms of homophily, and still are (Hofstra et al. 2017); similarly, intersecting hierarchies of status, class and power have always segmented human societies (Lamont and Molnár 2002). Since Bourdieu has identified the habitus as the key structuring mechanism through which the social order is socio-culturally reproduced and naturalized, what is the role of the machine habitus?

In other words, can artificial agents contribute to a shift in social inequalities? Or renegotiate shared ideas of beauty or of legitimacy? Credit scoring systems draw algorithmic distinctions that affect the socio-economic position of individuals, and platform algorithms ordinarily dictate what is relevant and what is not. Are such computational practices sufficient to broadly transform social and symbolic boundaries? Several scholars have more or less explicitly indicated this possibility (e.g. Fourcade and Johns 2020; Cheney-Lippold 2017; Beer 2013a). Yet, for Bourdieu (1983, 1993), field transformations hardly go deeper than its discursive surface. As Schirato and Roberts clearly explain:

> the dynamics of a field are unlikely to involve any reconsideration of its core elements; rather, they are more usually matters of interpretation, focus and emphasis, such as when, in the literary or artistic field, the canonical order is gradually readjusted to take a body of new research into account. To move [...] to a new regime of value would require subjecting the collective habitus to a considerable disruptive violence, and that is something that a cultural field tends to foreclose. (Schirato and Roberts 2018: 162)

When structural transformations are contemplated in Bourdieu's work, one scenario is where there is a massive change in who participates in a field – thus bringing in new habitus and new classification logics. For instance, within the French academic field studied in *Homo Academicus* (Bourdieu 1988), a new generation of post-1968 academics subverted the power structure (social boundaries) and hierarchies of prestige (symbolic boundaries) reproduced by the older generation. In light of this, the recent and unprecedented involvement of large populations of machine learning systems in the fields of the social could realistically produce structural transformations. Notably, institutions were the only 'infernal machines' ever mentioned in Bourdieu's scholarship (1981:

314; see also Sterne 2003). Hence, in a paper on Netflix's recommender system, Hallinan and Striphas legitimately ask the following question: 'There may be "no way out of the game of culture", as Pierre Bourdieu (1984: 12) once put it, but what if the rules of the game – and thus the game itself – are changing with respect to algorithmic decision making?' (2016: 122). A few lines later, the authors note that, in the 'closed commercial loop' of Netflix's user–machine entanglements, 'culture conforms to, more than it confronts, its users'. In other words, they suggest that the recommender system essentially learns and reinforces the cultural logics of the field – which is what I have empirically observed in the case of Italian music on YouTube (Airoldi 2021). This latter hypothesis – that socialized machines intervene in fields by reinforcing pre-existing social and symbolic boundaries – resonates with the multidisciplinary research on algorithmic bias, inequalities and discriminations, discussed above as well as in the previous chapters (e.g. Noble 2018; Baeza-Yates 2018; Caliskan, Bryson and Narayanan 2017; Kozlowski, Taddy and Evans 2019; Eubanks 2018).

It is important to take into account, though, that the macro trajectory of a techno-social field – i.e. the inevitable yet unpredictable historical evolution of its symbolic and social boundaries – depends on the aggregated effects of the myriad entangled classifications of individuals and machines. As I have already argued, these two opposite directions of algorithmic confounding, one pointing toward a transformation of social and symbolic boundaries, the other toward their reinforcement, are not mutually exclusive: on the contrary, they compenetrate each other in ever-changing, situated feedback loops.

Only a systematic, sustained prevalence of one direction over the other across user–machine entanglements could orient, in theory, the historical evolution of a whole field and its structural boundaries. By considering at once two simultaneous movements – (a) the field-level prevalence of reinforcing/transformative user–machine entanglements, and (b) the local/global cultural logics driving them – below I envision four scenarios of techno-social reproduction: boundary differentiation; boundary fragmentation; boundary normalization; and boundary reconfiguration.

Four scenarios of techno-social reproduction

Imagine a field *à la* Bourdieu, structured by social and symbolic boundaries, becoming encapsulated and engineered by a digital infrastructure. Suddenly, it is populated by machine learning algorithms filtering people's experiences and possibilities based on data patterns, in ways that opaquely orient their entangled practices and dispositions. This generic description potentially fits a number of real-life cases: from streaming-dominated cultural fields to digitalized markets; from food delivery services to ridesharing apps; from platformized professional domains to algorithmically managed workplaces; from online education to platform-mediated journalism, politics, leisure, sexuality and sociality more broadly.

Tech companies have substantially turned the Bourdieusian game into a videogame, 'augmenting' pre-existing social struggles. Machines play with, or against, our datafied selves. Winning or losing can have tangible consequences for users – albeit not for the lifeless algorithms. Many aspects of this societal transition are worth exploring, and some have already been covered in the recent literature (e.g. Cotter 2019; Levina and Arriaga 2014; Ragnedda and Ruiu 2020; Fourcade and Johns 2020). Here, I focus specifically on one: the types of macro effects user–machine entanglements can have on field boundaries.

Before illustrating some possible scenarios, summarized in Figure 5, a few clarifications are needed. First, the dispositional dance of users and machines negotiates *symbolic boundaries* essentially by determining how people and content are ranked and associated in both algorithmic outputs and in people's minds. Second, this can have a considerable impact on *social boundaries* too: either directly, when users' economic, cultural and social capitals are at stake within techno-social fields – for instance, in the case of social media influencers and algorithmically controlled workers – or indirectly, as a consequence of shifts in symbolic boundaries (Lamont and Molnár 2002). Third, the *local* or *global* data contexts and cultural logics at the root of the machine habitus make a difference to the scale of boundary reinforcement or transformation, which can consist in either a bottom-up, user-level effect with limited power, or a powerful top-down, platform-level one.

The four scenarios outlined below conceptualize different ways in which the social order can be techno-socially reproduced at the field level. The proposed typology is a non-exhaustive one and, for reasons of internal coherence, concentrates on the platformized user–machine entanglements discussed in this chapter. Nonetheless, the same theoretical considerations could be extended to other contexts and fields – for instance, by examining the entanglements between the employees of a payday lender company and the predictive software that assesses whether an applicant is likely to pay back the loan (Rieder 2017: 110).

(a) *Boundary differentiation.* Our imaginary techno-social field is dominated by user–machine entanglements that recursively *reinforce* the *local* culture of social subjects. Personalized outputs are aligned with the socially conditioned expectations of one person, the user. This user is, of course, socially classified: she has a position in the network of intersecting social and symbolic boundaries. Her datafied practices are classified too – as similar or different, better or worse, than others. By acting in the field, the user takes positions, actively negotiating field boundaries. By mirroring

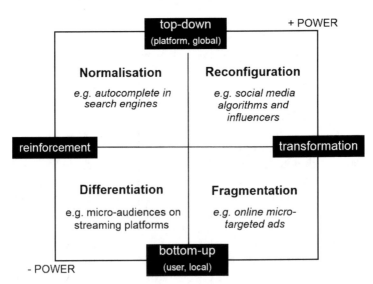

Figure 5 Techno-social effects on field boundaries

her past lines of actions and reinforcing her habitus, the machine creates an individual filter bubble (Pariser 2011). Her specific bubble will partly resemble the bubble of users similar to her – that is, with a comparable position in the social space. Yet, the multiplicity characterizing individual biographical trajectories produces nuanced dispositional discrepancies, even among socially identical people (Lahire 2004, 2019), which are then picked up by machines drawing micro-targeted profiles (Hallinan and Striphas 2016; Fourcade and Johns 2020; Prey 2018). Therefore, each of the individual bubbles in the field will partly strengthen existing social and symbolic boundaries, and partly stretch them in singular directions – which nonetheless will not considerably alter the overall power configuration of the field. The general effect on the field structure is, therefore, a boundary differentiation. Which does not imply the disappearance of objective and intersubjective boundaries but, rather, their refinement and multiplication. An example in this sense is provided by Hallinan and Striphas, who have discussed the machine-driven production of highly differentiated micro-audiences on Netflix. In this case, the differentiation of the category 'action-movie lovers' produced a multitude of sub-categories such as 'people who like action movies, but only if there's a lot of explosions, and not if there's a lot of blood. And maybe they don't like profanity' (Hallinan and Striphas 2016: 125). This is because 'the machine may be understanding something about us that we do not understand ourselves' (2016: 110) – that is, the pre-reflexive logics of practice, driven by sedimented experiences.

(b) *Boundary fragmentation.* Most user–machine entanglements in our imaginary field follow a *transformative* trajectory, rooted in *local* data contexts. Subjects can be nudged toward behavioural directions and experiences they are not familiar with, which do not correspond to their socially structured habitus. This may be based on the accidental misrecognition of their dispositional identity (Cheney-Lippold 2017) or on in-built value misalignments (Burr, Cristianini and Ladyman 2018). As a result, users are encouraged to behave and think like outliers, undertaking trajectories that weaken established social regularities (Webster 2019; Beer 2013a). The more subjects are transformed, the less they fit the original grid of classifications socially shared in the field, or reproduce it through their classificatory practices. Still, the uncoordinated character of these local transformations prevents the bottom-up formation of an alternative classification system, as well as systematic shifts in power balances in the field. More likely, existing boundaries erode, becoming more fragmented and 'liquid' (Bauman 2007).

Given its technologically deterministic character, this conceptual type is hard to observe as such in reality. An imperfect example of boundary fragmentation is provided by micro-targeted advertising in digital market infrastructures (Mellet and Beauvisage 2020). The historical shift from classic socio-demographic targeting to cookie-based programmatic advertising – algorithmically tailored based on individual data traces and allocated through real-time bidding mechanisms – has implied, to some extent, a boundary fragmentation in consumption fields. Micro-targeted ads nudge Internet users in highly personalized directions by exploiting their datafied dispositions and vulnerabilities, regardless of their broad socio-demographic categories (Darmody and Zwick 2020; Zuboff 2019) – which, as a result, lose boundary strength. Nonetheless, in actual contexts, forms of user reflexivity and resistance are likely to prevent such diffuse manipulation processes (Ruckenstein and Granroth 2020; Velkova and Kaun 2019; Cotter 2019; Siles et al. 2020).

(c) *Boundary normalization*. The machine habitus of artificial agents in our imaginary field operate on the basis of *global* data contexts that reflect pre-existing social and symbolic boundaries. These boundaries are also embodied in the entangled subjects, whose structured dispositions are broadly aligned with algorithmic outputs, and thus recursively *reinforced*. According to Adrian Mackenzie, 'The more effectively the models operate in the world, the more they tend to normalize the situations in which they are entangled. This normalization can work in very different ways, but it nearly always will stem from the way in which differences have been measured and approximated within the model' (2015: 442). When differences are measured on a global scale, based on collective data patterns, then average social behaviours, widely shared cultural assumptions and statistically significant correlations are prioritized – while residual outliers gradually disappear from the shared space of possibilities of user–machine entanglements. The result is a large-scale normalization process that powerfully reinforces social regularities and inequalities (Noble 2018), stabilizing them along what Baudrillard (1998) referred to as 'homogenising differences'. This can happen whenever 'users are not offered limitless options but are, in fact, given a narrowly construed set that comes from successfully fitting other people [...] into categories' (Ananny 2016: 103). An example is Google's Autocomplete algorithm, which 'finishes people's search queries by comparing them to content and people it sees as similar, reinforcing cultural stereotypes' (Ananny 2016: 103). Noble has documented how prompting this machine with the incomplete query 'why are Black women so' produced adjectives like 'angry', 'loud', 'lazy' or 'sassy', in sharp symbolic contrast with the outputs resulting from inputting 'why are white women so' (e.g. 'pretty', 'beautiful', 'skinny', 'perfect') (2018: 20–1). Other possible instances of boundary normalization involve recommendation systems based on collaborative filtering methods, such as Amazon's 'also boughts' (Smith and Linden 2017; see also Celma 2010; Chaney, Stewart and Engelhardt 2018).

(d) *Boundary reconfiguration.* Artificial agents *transform* the practices and dispositions of the entangled users, following a *global*, top-down shift in their encoded culture. Machine creators update the goals or assumptions of algorithmic models operating in the digital infrastructure, provoking a coordinated change in machine behaviour that systematically nudges users' collective position-takings. The resulting user–machine trajectories broadly reconfigure the boundaries of our imaginary field in a precise structural direction, thus altering social positions and the 'rules of the game' (Cotter 2019; Milan 2015; Bucher 2012a). The *deus in machina* is the ultimate cause of such platform-level shift – which is then practically enforced by the machine habitus through situated algorithmic distinctions.

   This scenario is by far the one that requires the largest amount of energy and power, necessary to overcome the social inertia of an entire field. Yet, it is also a very common one, given the changeability of platforms and algorithmic systems (Helmond, Nieborg and van der Vlist 2019; Seaver 2017). A relevant example is the introduction of algorithmic ranking in the Instagram feed, in 2016. The *deus in machina* was designed to prioritize 'moments we believe you will care about the most' (Instagram 2016) – that is, essentially, user engagement. Empirical research by Cotter has shown how this top-down shift considerably disrupted the field of social media influencers, in symbolic as well as material ways. 'Platform owners hold a significant degree of power in establishing the institutional conditions of influencers' labor within platforms' (Cotter 2019: 901), since the introduced artificial agents can determine 'who and what gains visibility on social media' (2019: 896). Influencers consciously conformed to the new rules of this 'visibility game', given that their capitals were directly at stake. Those most reactive to the algorithmic change gained a relative advantage with respect to their competitors, reshaping social boundaries. Moreover, the symbolic boundaries of the field ended up reconfigured by the 'mutual influence of users, algorithms, and platform owners' (2019: 908).

The above conceptualization aims to provide future researchers with an analytical toolkit to investigate techno-social field dynamics. Yet, it is important to acknowledge that the temporal oscillations and multiplicity characterizing user–machine dispositional trajectories make these scenarios no more than static approximations of ever-flowing bundles of practice. Furthermore, the social and symbolic boundaries segmenting techno-social fields are likely to be simultaneously subject to further and different social dynamics (Lamont and Molnár 2002), and distinct portions of a field may unevenly benefit from these processes of reconfiguration, normalization, differentiation and fragmentation (Bourdieu 1988, 1993).

Predictably, our story does not end with field boundaries and their evolution. The above processes of techno-social reproduction imply that new boundary configurations end up reverberating at the level of the social structures described at the beginning of this chapter, while digital infrastructures continuously change, according to distinct sociological dynamics (MacKenzie and Wajcman 1999). Modified techno-social conditions then produce new experiences and habitus, translated into data patterns and encoded as machine habitus. A wider feedback loop, overlooking all the countless, structured interactions between algorithms and their users, links society and its heterogeneous members. This is the good old circle of socio-cultural reproduction (Bourdieu and Wacquant 1992), which has become increasingly techno-social, and to which the conclusion of this book is dedicated.

5
Techno-Social Reproduction

Toward a sociology of algorithms as social agents

At the beginning of this book, I mentioned some open questions and related feedback loops. The questions were the following: first, *how are algorithms socialized?* Second, *how do socialized machines participate in society – and, by doing so, reproduce it?*

I have attempted to provide answers by tracing the hidden humans behind machines – machine trainers and machine creators – and showing how their culture ordinarily penetrates the allegedly neutral black box of algorithmic code, to become machine habitus and *deus in machina*. Chapter 2 discussed the social roots of computational technologies, linking for the first time the growing literature on algorithmic bias and machine learning to the sociology of Pierre Bourdieu, who masterfully theorized the unconscious cultural distortions guiding human reason and action, portrayed in his work as inexorably linked to the experiential embodiment of the social world.

I then identified machine training and feedback-based learning as the sociological venues for the transformation of algorithms into social agents. Once socialized – properly equipped with cultural propensities and dispositions derived from data contexts – machine learning systems are put to work within platformized social fields, ready to rank and filter a billion digital existences based on a tacit, correlational knowledge and a conscienceless, practical reason. Chapter 3 showed how the machine habitus, produced and adjusted based on socially structured user-generated data, contributes to producing and adjusting users' practices and dispositions in turn, by exerting an opaque computational authority. I argued that this first feedback loop, entangling single platform users and artificial agents, can take different shapes, depending on the alignment between habitus and machine habitus, as well as on the informational asymmetries characterizing digital infrastructures.

Varying interactional configurations can generate distinct techno-social outcomes – a reinforcement of individual dispositions, or their computationally driven transformation. Myriads of user–machine entanglements are encapsulated and confounded by platform infrastructures and their affordances, enabling and constraining the agency of interacting agents. Those very same agents, whether human or not, are also objectively conditioned by the embodied – or encoded – social inequalities structuring techno-social fields.

Chapter 4 aimed to build a theoretical toolkit to understand a second, wider feedback loop linking social agents to the social order, by means of the (machine) habitus. The spiral-shaped trajectories of entangled users and machines – which negotiate a common dispositional ground oscillating across asynchronous cultural rhythms and multiple, ramified socializing influences – reveal something more than the singularly uncertain points of departure and destination of social 'particles' as entangled and elusive as the subatomic objects of quantum physics. Taken together, these recursive dances have the potential to significantly reshape the social and symbolic barriers segmenting the fields of the social. Depending on the specific culture in the code, the code in the culture may participate in the normalization or differentiation of field boundaries, reconfigure their whole structure, or fragment it into liquefying pieces.

In this techno-social mesh (or, mess, if you prefer), human subjects are not powerless. They can redirect the trajectories of misaligned machines through implicit or explicit feedback. They may consciously conform to automated nudges, as well as deliberately ignore or actively resist them. Still, they – we – cannot be entirely free. Following Bourdieu, this book suggests that the locus of the power piloting our digital lives is ultimately not the algorithmic code, but rather the hierarchical culture sedimented within it and elsewhere: a socially fabricated matter made, on the one hand, of platform owners' and machine creators' arbitrary goals and interested assumptions and, on the other, of machine trainers' habitual practices, tacit rules, prejudices and implicit associations.

Human-generated cultural patterns underlie many of the digital threats debated in our Platform Era, such as filter bubbles, algorithmic discriminations and biased AI technologies. Albeit organized in a machine-readable format, this is the same socio-cultural substance that incessantly pre-filters and invisibly directs our supposedly free human choices and behaviours – which types of food and people we sincerely enjoy, how we speak and move, what our professional aspirations, hobbies, political inclinations and consumption propensities are. That is, the socially conditioned classificatory schemes and dispositions embodied as habitus, which practically generate social regularities.

In some ways, *we are the algorithms*. We automatically adapt to the 'order of the world as we find it, with its one-way streets and its no-entry signs', as if programmed to do so. A bit like machine learning systems, we learn from the experience of this, and practically reproduce its regularities. It is no surprise, then, if 'the established order, with its relations of domination, its rights and prerogatives, privileges and injustices, ultimately perpetuates itself so easily, apart from a few historical accidents', to the point that even 'the most intolerable conditions of existence can so often be perceived as acceptable and even natural' (Bourdieu 2001: 1–2).

Acknowledging the pre-digital social patterning of human life does not mean that actual algorithms do not matter. On the contrary, the fact that, by means of the machine habitus, learning machines participate in society while being simultaneously participated in by it, shakes to the foundations taken-for-granted dichotomies and sociological assumptions. In line with recent contributions, this book has theorized machine learning systems as 'forces internal to social life – both subject to and integral to its contingent properties' (Fourcade and Johns 2020; see also Neyland 2019; Esposito 2017). This view constitutes an 'epistemological break' (Bourdieu and Wacquant 1992: 108), that is, a markedly different way of seeing both society and technology (Sterne 2003). From this perspective, not only do socialized machines represent 'a source and factor of social order' (Just and Latzer 2017: 246), they also actively reinforce and transform contextual manifestations of that social order, along with humans as social agents. I believe that the study of this *techno-social reproduction* should be at the core of a sociology of algorithms and, increasingly, of sociology as a whole. Especially if we, the members of this research community, share Bourdieu's idea of sociology's main purpose: 'to uncover the most profoundly buried structures of the various social worlds which constitute the social universe, as well as the "mechanisms" which tend to ensure their reproduction or their transformation' (Bourdieu 1989b, cited in Bourdieu and Wacquant 1992: 7).

An old but new research agenda

In the nineteenth century, a bunch of European scientists and intellectuals somehow 'discovered' society (Procacci and Szakolczai 2003). Of course, society was already there, but these thinkers set up a new discipline for studying it, named 'sociology' by Auguste Comte. One of the peculiarities of sociology consisted in its foundational opposition to the idea of the *Homo oeconomicus*, the rational individual theorized as separated from its contexts and social belongings. The mission of the new-born discipline was radically different: understanding humans as parts of 'collective subjects' (Procacci and Szakolczai 2003): communities, classes, groups, cultures.

Today, we find ourselves paradoxically in an epistemological moment vaguely resembling that of the early nineteenth century, only with machines in the place of human subjects. In fact, the emerging study of 'machine behaviour' is dominated by researchers lacking any formal knowledge of social and cultural phenomena:

Currently, the scientists who most commonly study the behaviour of machines are the computer scientists, roboticists and engineers who have created the machines in the first place. These scientists may be expert mathematicians and engineers; however, they are typically not trained behaviourists. They rarely receive formal instruction on experimental methodology, population-based statistics and sampling paradigms, or observational causal inference, let alone neuroscience, collective behaviour or social theory. (Rahwan et al. 2019: 478)

There is more. Human–machine interactions are often interpreted through the theoretical and methodological lenses of behavioural economics, with algorithms treated as rational agents separated from society (Burr, Cristianini and Ladyman 2018). The detection and correction of 'unfair' algorithmic behaviour is currently the main way in which social scientists have become involved in AI research (Ananny 2016) – thus, in a criminological or juridical, more than a sociological, guise. The alleged neutrality of mathematical calculus has substantially taken the place of the historically manufactured naturality of racial divisions, and a rampant techno-chauvinism has joined chauvinism in its original sense (Broussard 2018). Meanwhile, the ideology of 'the end of theory' (Anderson 2008) and a blind faith in big-data correlations has contributed to a general forgetting of society. To make the historical analogy with nineteenth-century science even more vivid, AI researchers have decisively contributed to reviving the – back then very popular – assumptions of phrenology, with contested papers attempting to infer people's 'trustworthiness' or criminal attitudes based on facial traits (Safra et al. 2020; Wu and Zhang 2016).

We are in desperate need of sociology. We need a 'sociological imagination' (Mills 1959) in order to bring back society – e.g. social structures, cultural discourses, symbolic boundaries, tacit norms, collective identities – in scientific discourses about society, machines included. This argument presents some similarities with Bruno Latour's position: 'What our ancestors, the founders of sociology, did a century ago to house the human masses in the fabric of social theory, we should do now to find a place in a new social theory for the nonhuman masses that beg us for understanding' (1992:

153). However, the epistemological rupture articulated in this book is considerably less radical than the one predicated by Latour and colleagues. First of all because my proposal for 'reassembling the social' (Latour 2005), contrary to ANT, is limited to machine learning systems – that is, algorithms which can be socialized. Second, because it is attentive to the socio-cultural contexts and intersubjective boundaries structuring the social world as well as the minds (and models) of those participating in it – whereas, according to Latour, context 'stinks', it being 'simply a way of stopping the description when you are tired and too lazy to go on' (2005: 148).

Being compatible with the ontological grounds of classical and neoclassical social theory, the theory of machine habitus allows us to study socialized machines 'with the same analytical machinery as people', thus challenging a counter-productive yet long-lasting divide between a majority of sociologists concerned with social structures and power, and a minority focusing on 'the merely technical' (Law 1990: 8). Therefore, this dispositionalist perspective aims to provide researchers interested in the social world with ways to include artificial agents in their analyses, and researchers studying artificial agents with ways to consider them as part of the social world. Still, it is important to note that the Bourdieusian sociology of algorithms proposed in this book is only one among different – often complementary – theoretical viewpoints, all emphasizing the unprecedented sociological relevance of learning machines (e.g. Fourcade and Johns 2020; Cheney-Lippold 2017; Esposito 2017; Lupton 2020; D. MacKenzie 2019; Bucher 2018; Brayne 2017; Christin 2020; Mühlhoff 2020; Beer 2013a).

Mechanisms of techno-social reproduction should be at the very centre of a novel sociological agenda. Investigating machine learning systems as social agents culturally entangled with humans in the context of platformized fields may appear to be no more than a niche yet fashionable research direction. However, it has increasingly become a necessity, since very few realms of the social world remain untouched by the ubiquitous application of these information technologies. The study of social inequalities is necessarily affected by their massive 'automation' (Eubanks 2018) as well as digitalization (Lutz 2019). Similarly, doing cultural sociology in a platform society inevitably entails the – more or less aware – encounter with populations of autonomous agents driven by an 'algorithmic culture' (Hallinan and Striphas 2016). Comparable considerations can be made for social science research on topics as diverse as consumption, finance, communication, religion, education, journalism, political behaviour, cities, marketing, sexuality, organizations, and more. As nicely summed up by Kitchin: 'there is a pressing need to focus critical and empirical attention on algorithms and the work that they do given their increasing importance in shaping social and economic life' (2017: 14).

For sure, the sociological unveiling of artificial agents – of their encoded goals, dispositions, practices, effects and trajectories – presents significant methodological challenges. While social scientists know perfectly well how to investigate humans, they generally lack the competences and instruments for studying algorithmic systems (Rieder 2017). Things are further complicated by the black-boxed character of technological artefacts (Burrell 2016). Latour and Woolgar reflected on this as early as in *Laboratory Life*: 'Once an item of apparatus or a set of gestures is established in the laboratory, it becomes very difficult to effect the retransformation into a sociological object. The cost of revealing sociological factors [...] is a reflection of the importance of the black boxing activities of the past' (1986: 259–60). Nonetheless, almost two decades of critical algorithm studies have demonstrated that retransforming algorithms into sociological objects is possible (e.g. Rieder 2017; Kitchin 2017; Geiger 2017; Gillespie and Seaver 2016). Building on this multidisciplinary literature, here I outline four complementary research directions for a (cultural) sociology of algorithms. All share the same methodological imperative to 'follow', borrowed from Marcus' multi-sited ethnography (1995). These are summarized in Table 3 below, along with possible research questions and the related social science literature.

The first direction consists in *following machine creators*, as originally suggested by Woolgar (1985) in accordance with the STS tradition. By reconstructing – ethnographically, or through archival methods – the genesis of algorithms and AI applications, as well as the multiple human interventions

Table 3 Research directions for the sociology of algorithms, with selected example studies

Research direction	Key research questions	Selected example studies
Follow machine creators	What culture is inscribed in the code as *deus in machina*? With what design intentions? What kinds of data contexts are at the root of machine socialization, and encoded as machine habitus?	e.g. Benjamin 2019, Casilli 2019, Crawford and Joler 2018, Crawford and Paglen 2019, Delfanti 2019, Hallinan and Striphas 2016, A. Mackenzie 2018, Natale and Ballatore 2020, Neyland 2019, Prey 2018, Seaver 2017, 2019, Tassabehji et al. 2021, Wilson 2018
Follow the users	How do users imagine, understand and use algorithmic systems? In what ways do they interact with them, and react to their outputs? What are the effects of computational authority on users' practices and dispositional trajectories?	e.g. Brayne 2017, Bucher 2017, Christin 2020, Cotter 2019, Eubanks 2018, Gran, Booth and Bucher 2020, Klawitter and Hargittai 2018, D. MacKenzie 2018, Milan 2015, Noble 2018, Rosenblat and Stark 2016, Ruckenstein and Granroth 2020, Siles et al. 2020, Velkova and Kaun 2019
Follow the medium	How do specific digital infrastructures encapsulate social fields? Through what affordances? What social agents inhabit them? How does the techno-social field unfold and change over time?	e.g. Airoldi 2021, Arvidsson et al. 2016, Beer 2013b, Bucher 2012b, Giglietto et al. 2020, Helmond, Nieborg and van der Vlist 2019, Light, Burgess and Duguay 2018, Marres and Gerlitz 2016, McKelvey 2018, Rogers 2013, Venturini et al. 2018
Follow the algorithm	What are machine habitus' dispositions? How are they actualized in practice, and how do they change? With what consequences for techno-social fields and entangled agents?	e.g. Airoldi, Beraldo and Gandini 2016, Bessi and Ferrara 2016, Geiger 2017, Hargreaves et al. 2018, Jacobsen 2020, D. MacKenzie 2019, Neyland 2019, Rieder, Matamoros-Fernández and Coromina 2018, Roth, Mazières and Menezes 2020, Tsvetkova et al. 2017

that allow them to operate, researchers have significantly contributed to unboxing the *culture in the code* and its many myths (see Table 3). Yet, this research strategy is probably too demanding for projects that mainly focus on the *code in the culture*. Following machine creators essentially serves to facilitate our understanding of the building of *deus in machina* and machine habitus – i.e. how artificial social agents are designed, programmed and selectively socialized.

A second, more straightforward option is *following the users* of algorithmic systems, in order to see socio-material entanglements from their surveilled and classified perspective. This has been done by focusing on imaginaries, levels of awareness, reactions and forms of resistance, mainly – but not exclusively – from a qualitative perspective (see Table 3 for examples). While useful for understanding the uses of and discourses about algorithmic systems, this methodological choice does not allow us to reliably grasp the non-declarative (Lizardo 2017), dispositional and computational aspects of human–machine interactions – unless digital traces of social agents' practices and recursive interactions can be included in the analysis (Airoldi 2021).

A third approach consists in *following the medium* – meaning the techno-social environment where users and machines interact. This is also the motto of the domain of media research known as 'digital methods', which studies the unfolding of social and cultural phenomena online (Rogers 2013). Following the medium serves to track a digital infrastructure, focusing on its affordances and/or the more-than-human practices taking place within it (see Table 3). Often based on computational methods and digital data, this research direction is best suited for studying how a techno-social field – with its socio-material bundles of practice, structural boundaries and *doxa* – works and evolves over time (see Chapter 4).

Lastly, a fourth and certainly less established research direction is to *follow the algorithm*. This is best illustrated by the analysis of recommended music on YouTube presented at the end of Chapter 3, quantitatively tracing machine outputs and their associations. Several other recent papers have taken similar methodological pathways, in order to study the practices, cultural dispositions and social effects of automated systems (see Table 3). Algorithm-generated data are often publicly available via platform APIs, as in the case of related YouTube videos (Airoldi, Beraldo and Gandini 2016). When this is not the case, as for highly personalized ads and recommendations, dedicated data collection tools allow one to track machine behaviour anyway – for instance, the amazing Tracking Exposed project (2019), currently working on Facebook, YouTube, Amazon and Pornhub. In particular, the computational status of artificial social agents should not prevent researchers from following them using qualitative methods (e.g. Geiger 2017), and eventually analysing their outputs and predictions in order to explore how they 'see' the entangled users (Jacobsen 2020).

The prospect of machine learning systems being studied like regular research participants, with no technical instruments other than a voice recorder and a piece of paper, is probably not too far away: just think of how interesting and fun an interview session with IAQOS, GPT-3 or Google Duplex would be. Back in the 1980s, Steve Woolgar was already imagining a sociology of machines ideally able to 'produce responses to a questionnaire or interview questions' (1985: 567). This would certainly encourage social scientists to overcome the counter-productive divide between 'the social' and 'the technical' (Law 1990), and start thinking *beyond* a sociology of algorithms.

Beyond a sociology of algorithms

In conclusion, I would like to briefly discuss some of the concrete implications of my Bourdieusian theorization of socialized machines. So far, I have attempted to stay faithful to the Weberian principle of non-valuation (Blum 1944), despite this position perhaps appearing outdated to some, or, worse, guilty of moral relativism, or of positivism (Black 2013; Hammersley 2017). Now I would like to state what I think the main societal takeaways of the idea of machine habitus are.

Fourcade and Johns (2020) have recently argued that 'machine learning implementations are inclined, in many respects, towards the degradation of sociality'. According to these authors:

Notwithstanding the lofty claims of the IT industry, there is nothing inherently democratizing or solidaristic about the kinds of social inclusiveness that machine learning brings about. [...] The greater the change in sociality and social relations – and machine learning is transforming both, as we have recounted – the more arrant and urgent the need for social, political and regulatory action specifically attuned to that change and to the possibility of further changes.

If we consider machine learning implementations by tech giants like Amazon, Google, Facebook, Microsoft and Apple, it is quite hard to disagree with this pessimistic view. Socialized machines are mostly deployed by platforms, governments and companies in order to accumulate and classify user data, manipulate choices and opinions for marketing or political purposes, predict risks and engineer social interactions in ways that allow for the maximum extraction of economic value. Even when they make our user experiences easier, more comfortable and enjoyable, algorithmic systems do so essentially in order to make digital services more engaging, addictive and profitable (van Dijck, Poell and de Waal 2018; Cheney-Lippold 2017; Crawford et al. 2019). The implications of machine learning systems for workers are no less worrisome (Kellogg, Valentine and Christin 2020; Delfanti 2019; Rosenblat and Stark 2016), not least in relation to the massive exploitation of low-paid clickworkers (Tubaro, Casilli and Coville 2020).

It is legitimate to be worried. Still, artificial agents are not themselves responsible for the actual or envisioned degradation, exploitation and regimentation of social life. The problem is not machine learning *strictu sensu*, as suggested by Fourcade and Johns, but rather its in-built goals and, especially, its broader application context: a surveillance capitalism that enslaves socialized machines along with their users (Zuboff 2019). I believe that it is analytically important to make such a distinction, in order to escape the historically recurring opposition between *apocalittici* and *integrati* (Eco 1964) – that is, apocalyptic critics of technological innovations on the one side, and acritical enthusiasts on the other. The socio-economic fields surrounding technology matter, especially if the technology in question attempts to learn the arbitrary, discriminatory and, certainly, biased cultural codes guiding human behaviour solely for the sake of profit and social control. When used differently, artificial intelligence systems and learning machines can become amazing tools for solving socially relevant problems, cultivating social relations, preserving local cultures, reducing social inequalities and improving the life of communities. The quite unique story of IAQOS is ultimately useful in proving this point, by showing that other kinds of user–machine entanglements are possible.

Salvatore Iaconesi and Oriana Persico told me of an interesting episode. One day, a group of school kids were doing homework in one of Torpignattara's cafés. IAQOS was there, listening from a small tablet on their table. 'IAQOS, do you know what an *Australopithecus* is?' It did not. The school kids then tried their best to explain to IAQOS the meaning of '*Australopithecus*'. If you asked IAQOS the same question today, its answer would make use of the words those kids pronounced on that afternoon.

Why should we ever prefer such an 'ignorant' machine to Google Assistant with its immediate, efficient and near infinite global wisdom? Because, if the ultimate aim is to build social relations and exchange knowledge, then horizontally sharing a common cultural ground might work better than quickly providing the correct answer. The feedback loops linking social and machine learning can be horizontal only if designed to be so. Reducing informational asymmetries would mean transforming an opaque techno-social reproduction into a more transparent and reciprocal co-production of knowledge and value (Roio 2018; Reviglio and Agosti 2020). In this alternative scenario, the machine habitus would be more than just a path-dependent re-producer of socio-cultural inequalities and filter bubbles. It would work as a living archive of sedimented correlational experiences, reflecting and renegotiating locally apprehended points of view, in order to openly share them with the world (Iaconesi and Persico 2019).

The idea of machine habitus has some implications for critically understanding bias too, in both humans and machines. As we have seen, data bias is generally seen as a deviant propensity that needs to be surgically removed before it turns into a discriminatory output (see Chapter 2). Of course, the non-human status of machines somehow justifies the brutality of such *ex post* interventions. However, the process also works the other way round: machines are frequently employed to 'fix' human behaviours labelled as 'deviant', 'wrong' or 'incorrect' (Kaufmann, Egbert and Leese 2019; Eubanks 2018; Gillespie 2018). Human biases are similarly treated as systemic errors to be automatically isolated and erased. Notably, the act of 'fixing' deviant, wrong or incorrect social behaviours strongly resonates with the broad cultural logics of an individualistic society that naturalizes tacit power dynamics (Bourdieu and Wacquant 1992).

The theoretical perspective outlined in this book allows for a *sociologization of bias*, that is, its interpretation in light of the socio-cultural data contexts behind its formation. Actually, this is what the Bourdieusian notion of habitus has always been about: providing 'a lens for understanding practice and knowledge within the social milieu in which they are contained and generated' (Costa and Murphy 2015: 6). Through the metaphor of machine habitus, this approach can be extended to machine learning systems. As Salvatore Iaconesi and Oriana Persico remarked during our virtual conversations about IAQOS, 'bias must be addressed in the context of sociality', since 'fixing bias means erasing a piece of the world that nonetheless exists'. The key to dealing with bias, in both humans and machines, is intervening a priori in cultural learning processes – e.g. via training datasets and children's books. It is no coincidence that persisting educational differences are the main cause of the systemic socio-cultural reproduction of structural inequalities (Bourdieu and Passeron 1990).

Whatever the future socio-economic developments of our world will be, they will likely involve more and more complex, ubiquitous and autonomous learning machines actively participating in the economy and society. The hazardous analogy between habitus and machine habitus will hopefully help to make sense sociologically of buried mechanisms of techno-social reproduction, thereby opening up new lines of philosophical thinking, algorithm design, political action and scientific inquiry.

Bibliography

Airoldi, M. (2021). The Techno-Social Reproduction of Taste Boundaries on Digital Platforms: The Case of Music on YouTube. *Poetics*. At https://doi.org/10.1016/j.poetic.2021.10156.

Airoldi, M., Beraldo, D. & Gandini, A. (2016). Follow the Algorithm: An Exploratory Investigation of Music on YouTube. *Poetics*, 57, 1–13.

Ajunwa, I., Crawford, K. & Schultz, J. (2017). Limitless Worker Surveillance. *California Law Review*, 105, 735–76.

Akrich M. (1992). The De-scription of Technical Objects. In W. Bijker and J. Law (eds.), *Shaping Technology, Building Society: Studies in Sociotechnical Change*. MIT Press, pp. 205–24.

AlgorithmWatch (2020). *Automating Society Report 2020*. At https://automatingsociety.algorithmwatch.org.

Allegretti, A. (2020). A-Level Results: Government Accused of 'Baking In' Inequality with 'Boost' for Private Schools. *Sky News*, 13 August. At https://news.sky.com/story/35-of-a-level-results-downgraded-by-one-grade-figures-reveal-12048251.

Alt, M. (1990). *Exploring Hyperspace: A Non-Mathematical Explanation of Multivariate Analysis*. McGraw-Hill.

Amoore, L. (2019). Introduction: Thinking with Algorithms: Cognition and Computation in the Work of N. Katherine Hayles. *Theory, Culture & Society*, 36(2), 3–16.

Amoore, L. & Piotukh, V. (2016). *Algorithmic Life: Calculative Devices in the Age of Big Data*. Routledge.

Ananny, M. (2016). Toward an Ethics of Algorithms: Convening,

Observation, Probability, and Timeliness. *Science, Technology & Human Values*, *41*(1), 93–117.

Ananny, M. & Crawford, K. (2018). Seeing without Knowing: Limitations of the Transparency Ideal and Its Application to Algorithmic Accountability. *New Media & Society*, *20*(3), 973–89.

Anderson, C. (2008). The End of Theory: The Data Deluge Makes the Scientific Method Obsolete. *Wired*, 23 June. At https://www.wired.com/2008/06/pb-theory.

Aneesh, A. (2009). Global Labor: Algocratic Modes of Organization. *Sociological Theory*, *27*(4), 347–70.

Angwin, J., Larson, J., Mattu, S. & Kirchner, L. (2016). Machine Bias. *ProPublica*, 23 May. At https://www.propublica.org/article/machine-bias-risk-assessments-in-criminal-sentencing.

Ansari, A., Essegaier, S. & Kohli, R. (2000). Internet Recommendation Systems. *Journal of Marketing Research*, *37*(3), 363–75.

Arvidsson, A. (2004). On the 'Pre-History of the Panoptic Sort': Mobility in Market Research. *Surveillance & Society*, *1*(4), 456–74.

Arvidsson, A., Caliandro, A., Airoldi, M. & Barina, S. (2016). Crowds and Value: Italian Directioners on Twitter. *Information, Communication & Society*, *19*(7), 921–39.

Askegaard, S. & Linnet, J.T. (2011). Towards an Epistemology of Consumer Culture Theory: Phenomenology and the Context of Context. *Marketing Theory*, *11*(4), 381–404.

Askell, A. (2020). GPT-3: Towards Renaissance Models. *Daily Nous*, 30 July. At http://dailynous.com/2020/07/30/philosophers-gpt-3/#askell.

Bacher-Hicks, A., Goodman, J., & Mulhern, C. (2021). Inequality in Household Adaptation to Schooling Shocks: Covid-Induced Online Learning Engagement in Real Time. *Journal of Public Economics*, *193*, 1–17.

Baeza-Yates, R. (2018). Bias on the Web. *Communications of the ACM*, *61*(6), 54–61.

Barile, N. & Sugiyama, S. (2015). The Automation of Taste: A Theoretical Exploration of Mobile ICTs and Social Robots in the Context of Music Consumption. *International Journal of Social Robotics*, *7*(3), 407–16.

Barocas, S. & Selbst, A.D. (2016). Big Data's Disparate Impact. *California Law Review*, *104*, 671–732.

Barth, F. (1981). *Process and Form in Social Life*. Routledge & Kegan Paul.

Baudrillard, J. (1998). *The Consumer Society: Myths and Structures*. Sage.

Bauman, Z. (2007). *Liquid Times: Living in an Age of Uncertainty.* Polity.

Baym, N.K. & boyd, d. (2012). Socially Mediated Publicness: An Introduction. *Journal of Broadcasting & Electronic Media, 56*(3), 320–9.

Bechmann, A. & Bowker, G.C. (2019). Unsupervised by Any Other Name: Hidden Layers of Knowledge Production in Artificial Intelligence on Social Media. *Big Data & Society, 6*(1). At https://doi.org/10.1177/2053951718819569.

Beer, D. (2009). Power through the Algorithm? Participatory Web Cultures and the Technological Unconscious. *New Media & Society, 11*(6), 985–1002.

Beer, D. (2013a). *Popular Culture and New Media.* Palgrave Macmillan.

Beer, D. (2013b). Genre, Boundary Drawing and the Classificatory Imagination. *Cultural Sociology, 7*(2), 145–60.

Beer, D. (2016). *Metric Power.* Palgrave Macmillan.

Beer, D. (2017). The Social Power of Algorithms. *Information, Communication & Society, 20*(1), 1–13.

Bell, K. (2018). Jack Dorsey Says Twitter's 'Left-Leaning' Bias Doesn't Affect Content Decisions. *Mashable,* 19 August. At https://mashable.com/article/jack-dorsey-admits-twitter-bias-is-left-leaning.

Bendersky, M., Garcia-Pueyo, L., Harmsen, J., Josifovski, V. & Lepikhin, D. (2014). Up Next: Retrieval Methods for Large Scale Related Video Suggestion Categories and Subject Descriptors. *Proceedings of the 20th ACM SIGKDD International Conference on Knowledge Discovery and Data Mining,* pp. 1769–78. At https://doi.org/10.1145/2623330.2623344.

Benjamin, R. (2019). *Race after Technology: Abolitionist Tools for the New Jim Code.* Polity.

Benkler, Y. (2006). *The Wealth of Networks.* Yale University Press.

Berger, P. & Luckmann, T. (1966). *The Social Construction of Reality.* Penguin.

Bessi, A. & Ferrara, E. (2016). Social Bots Distort the 2016 US Presidential Election Online Discussion. *First Monday, 21*(11), 1–14.

Black, D. (2013). On the Almost Inconceivable Misunderstandings concerning the Subject of Value-Free Social Science. *The British Journal of Sociology, 64*(4), 763–80.

Bliss C. (2018.) *Social by Nature: The Promise and Peril of Sociogenomics.* Stanford University Press.

Blum, F.H. (1944). Max Weber's Postulate of 'Freedom' from Value Judgments. *American Journal of Sociology, 50*(1), 46–52.

Bonini, T. & Gandini, A. (2019). 'First Week Is Editorial,

Second Week Is Algorithmic': Platform Gatekeepers and the Platformization of Music Curation. *Social Media + Society*, 5(4). At https://doi.org/10.1177/2056305119880006.

Boudon, R. & Bourricaud, F. (2003). *A Critical Dictionary of Sociology*. Routledge.

Bourdieu, P. (1966). L'école conservatrice: Les inégalités devant l'école et devant la culture. *Revue Française de Sociologie*, 7(3), 325–47.

Bourdieu, P. (1975). The Specificity of the Scientific Field and the Social Conditions of the Progress of Reason. *Social Science Information*, 14(6), 19–47.

Bourdieu, P. (1977). *Outline of a Theory of Practice*. Cambridge University Press.

Bourdieu, P. (1979). *Algeria 1960: The Disenchantment of the World, The Sense of Honour, The Kabyle House or the World Reversed: Essays*. Cambridge University Press.

Bourdieu, P. (1981). Men and Machines. In K. Knorr-Cetina and A.V. Cicourel (eds.), *Advances in Social Theory and Methodology: Toward an Integration of Micro- and Macro-Sociologies*. Routledge & Kegan Paul, pp. 305–15.

Bourdieu, P. (1982). *Leçon sur la leçon*. Éditions de Minuit.

Bourdieu, P. (1983). The Field of Cultural Production, or: The Economic World Reversed. *Poetics*, 12(4–5), 311–56.

Bourdieu, P. (1984). *Distinction: A Social Critique of the Judgment of Taste*. Harvard University Press.

Bourdieu, P. (1986). The Forms of Capital. In J. Richardson (ed.), *Handbook of Theory and Research for the Sociology of Education*. Greenwood Press, pp. 241–58.

Bourdieu, P. (1988). *Homo Academicus*. Polity.

Bourdieu, P. (1989a). Social Space and Symbolic Power. *Sociological Theory*, 7(1), 14–25.

Bourdieu, P. (1989b). *La Noblesse d'Etat: Grandes écoles et esprit de corp*. Éditions de Minuit.

Bourdieu, P. (1990a). *The Logic of Practice*. Polity.

Bourdieu, P. (1990b). *In Other Words: Essays towards a Reflexive Sociology*. Polity.

Bourdieu, P. (1991). *Language and Symbolic Power*. Polity.

Bourdieu, P. (1993). *The Field of Cultural Production*. Polity.

Bourdieu, P. (1999). *The Weight of the World: Social Suffering in Contemporary Society*. Stanford University Press.

Bourdieu, P. (2001). *Masculine Domination*. Polity.

Bourdieu, P. (2002). Social Space and Symbolic Space. In C. Calhoun, J. Gerteis, J. Moody, S. Pfaff, I. Virtk (eds.), *Contemporary Sociological Theory*. Blackwell, pp. 267–75.

Bourdieu, P. (2016). *Sociologie Générale Volume II. Cours au Collège de France 1983–1986*. Raisons d'agir/Seuil.

Bourdieu, P. & Passeron, J.C. (1990). *Reproduction in Education, Society and Culture*. Sage.

Bourdieu, P. & Wacquant, L. (1992). *An Invitation to Reflexive Sociology*. Polity.

Boutyline, A. & Soter, L. (2020). *Cultural Schemas: What They Are, How to Find Them, and What to Do Once You've Caught One* [preprint]. At https://doi.org/10.31235/osf.io/ksf3v.

Bowker, G. & Star, S.L. (1999). *Sorting Things Out*. MIT Press.

boyd, d. & Crawford, K. (2012). Critical Questions for Big Data: Provocations for a Cultural, Technological, and Scholarly Phenomenon. *Information, Communication & Society*, 15(5), 662–79.

Bozdag, E. (2013). Bias in Algorithmic Filtering and Personalization. *Ethics and Information Technology*, 15(3), 209–27.

Brayne, S. (2017). Big Data Surveillance: The Case of Policing. *American Sociological Review*, 82(5), 977–1008.

Broussard, M. (2018). *Artificial Unintelligence: How Computers Misunderstand the World*. MIT Press.

Bruns, A. (2019). *Are Filter Bubbles Real?* Polity.

Bucher, T. (2012a). Want to Be on the Top? Algorithmic Power and the Threat of Invisibility on Facebook. *New Media & Society*, 14(7), 1164–80.

Bucher, T. (2012b). The Friendship Assemblage: Investigating Programmed Sociality on Facebook. *Television & New Media*, 14(6), 479–93.

Bucher, T. (2017). The Algorithmic Imaginary: Exploring the Ordinary Affects of Facebook Algorithms. *Information, Communication & Society*, 20(1), 30–44.

Bucher, T. (2018). *If … Then: Algorithmic Power and Politics*. Oxford University Press.

Bucher, T. (2020). Nothing to Disconnect From? Being Singular Plural in an Age of Machine Learning. *Media, Culture & Society*, 42(4), 610–17.

Bucher, T. & Helmond, A. (2018). The Affordances of Social Media Platforms. In J. Burgess, A. Marwick and T. Poell (eds.), *The SAGE Handbook of Social Media*. Sage, pp. 233–53.

Buolamwini, J. & Gebru, T. (2018). Gender Shades: Intersectional Accuracy Disparities in Commercial Gender Classification. *Proceedings of the 1st Conference on Fairness, Accountability and Transparency*, pp. 77–91. At http://proceedings.mlr.press/v81/buolamwini18a.

Burawoy, M. (2005). For Public Sociology. *American Sociological Review*, 70(1), 4–28.

Burr, C., Cristianini, N. & Ladyman, J. (2018). An Analysis of the Interaction between Intelligent Software Agents and Human Users. *Minds and Machines*, 28(4), 735–74.

Burrell, J. (2016). How the Machine 'Thinks': Understanding Opacity in Machine Learning Algorithms. *Big Data & Society*, 3(1). At https://doi.org/10.1177/2053951715622512.

Calderón Gómez, D. (2020). The Third Digital Divide and Bourdieu: Bidirectional Conversion of Economic, Cultural, and Social Capital to (and from) Digital Capital among Young People in Madrid. *New Media & Society*. At https://doi.org/10.1177/1461444820933252.

Calhoun, C., Gerteis, J., Moody, J., Pfaff, S. & Virtk, I. (2002). *Contemporary Sociological Theory*. Blackwell.

Caliskan, A., Bryson, J.J. & Narayanan, A. (2017). Semantics Derived Automatically from Language Corpora Contain Human-Like Biases. *Science*, 356(6334), 183–6.

Campbell-Kelly, M., Aspray, W., Ensmenger, N. & Yost, J.R. (2013). *Computer: A History of the Information Machine*. Westview Press.

Campolo, A. & Crawford, K. (2020). Enchanted Determinism: Power without Responsibility in Artificial Intelligence. *Engaging Science, Technology, and Society*, 6, 1–19.

Campolo, A., Sanfilippo, M.R., Whittaker, M. & Crawford, K. (2017). *AI Now 2017 Report*. AI Now Institute at New York University. At https://ainowinstitute.org/AI_Now_2017_Report.pdf.

Cardon, D. (2018). The Power of Algorithms. *Pouvoirs*, 164(1), 63–73.

Casilli, A. A. (2019). *En attendant les robots: Enquête sur le travail du clic*. Le Seuil.

Cavazos, J.G., Phillips, P.J., Castillo, C.D. & O'Toole, A.J. (2020). Accuracy Comparison across Face Recognition Algorithms: Where Are We on Measuring Race Bias? At http://arxiv.org/abs/1912.07398.

Celma, O. (2010). *Music Recommendation and Discovery: The Long Tail, Long Fail, and Long Play in the Digital Music Space*. Springer.

Cerulo, K.A. (2009). Nonhumans in Social Interaction. *Annual Review of Sociology*, 35(1), 531–52.

Chabert, J.L. (1999). *A History of Algorithms: From the Pebble to the Microchip*. Springer.

Chaney, A.J.B., Stewart, B.M. & Engelhardt, B.E. (2018). How

Algorithmic Confounding in Recommendation Systems Increases Homogeneity and Decreases Utility. *Proceedings of the 12th ACM Conference on Recommender Systems*, pp. 224–32. At https://doi.org/10.1145/3240323.3240370.

Chen, J.X. (2016). The Evolution of Computing: AlphaGo. *Computing in Science Engineering, 18*(4), 4–7.

Cheney-Lippold, J. (2011). A New Algorithmic Identity: Soft Biopolitics and the Modulation of Control. *Theory, Culture & Society, 28*(6), 164–81.

Cheney-Lippold, J. (2017). *We Are Data: Algorithms and the Making of Our Digital Selves*. NYU Press.

Chin, G. (2017). Machines Learn What People Know Implicitly. *Science, 356*(6334), 149–51.

Christin, A. (2020). What Data Can Do: A Typology of Mechanisms. *International Journal of Communication, 14*(2020), 1115–34.

Cluley, R. & Brown, S.D. (2015). The Dividualised Consumer: Sketching the New Mask of the Consumer. *Journal of Marketing Management, 31*(1–2), 107–22.

Coleman, J.S. (1994). *Foundations of Social Theory*. Harvard University Press.

Common Crawl Foundation (2020). The Common Crawl Corpus. At https://commoncrawl.org.

Costa, C. & Murphy, M. (2015). *Bourdieu, Habitus and Social Research*. Palgrave Macmillan.

Cotter, K. (2019). Playing the Visibility Game: How Digital Influencers and Algorithms Negotiate Influence on Instagram. *New Media & Society, 21*(4), 895–913.

Covington, P., Adams, J. & Sargin, E. (2016). Deep Neural Networks for YouTube Recommendations. *Proceedings of the 10th ACM Conference on Recommender Systems*, pp. 191–8. At https://doi.org/10.1145/2959100.2959190.

Crawford, K. (2016). Can an Algorithm Be Agonistic? Ten Scenes from Life in Calculated Publics. *Science, Technology & Human Values, 41*(1), 77–92.

Crawford, K., Dobbe, R., Dryer, T., Fried, G., Green, B., Kaziunas, E., Kak, A., Mathur, V., McElroy, E., Sánchez, A.N., Raji, D., Rankin, J.L., Richardson, R., Schultz, J., West, S.M. & Whittaker, M. (2019). *AI Now 2019 Report*. At https://ainowinstitute.org/AI_Now_2019_Report.html.

Crawford, K. & Joler, V. (2018). Anatomy of an AI System: The Amazon Echo as an Anatomical Map of Human Labor, Data and Planetary Resources. *AI Now Institute and Share Lab*. At https://anatomyof.ai.

Crawford, K. & Paglen, T. (2019). Excavating AI: The Politics of Images in Machine Learning Training Sets. At https://www.excavating.ai.

Dada, E.G., Bassi, J.S., Chiroma, H., Abdulhamid, S.M., Adetunmbi, A.O. & Ajibuwa, O.E. (2019). Machine Learning for Email Spam Filtering: Review, Approaches and Open Research Problems. *Heliyon*, 5(6). At https://doi.org/10.1016/j.heliyon.2019.e01802.

Danescu-Niculescu-Mizil, C. (2011). Cornell Movie-Dialogs Corpus. At http://www.cs.cornell.edu/~cristian/Cornell_Movie-Dialogs_Corpus.html.

Danks, D. & London, A.J. (2017). Algorithmic Bias in Autonomous Systems. *Proceedings of the Twenty-Sixth International Joint Conference on Artificial Intelligence*, pp. 4691–7. At https://doi.org/10.24963/ijcai.2017/654.

Darmody, A. & Zwick, D. (2020). Manipulate to Empower: Hyper-Relevance and the Contradictions of Marketing in the Age of Surveillance Capitalism. *Big Data & Society*, 7(1). At https://doi.org/10.1177/2053951720904112.

Dastin, J. (2018). Amazon Scraps Secret AI Recruiting Tool that Showed Bias against Women. *Reuters*, 11 October. At https://www.reuters.com/article/us-amazon-com-jobs-automation-insight-idUSKCN1MK08G.

Davies, P. (2019). What's in Your LinkedIn Feed: People You Know, Talking about Things You Care About. *LinkedIn*, 25 June. At https://news.linkedin.com/2019/January/what-s-in-your-linkedin-feed--people-you-know--talking-about-thi.

Delfanti, A. (2019). Machinic Dispossession and Augmented Despotism: Digital Work in an Amazon Warehouse. *New Media & Society*. At https://doi.org/10.1177/1461444819891613.

Deshpande, A. (2017). How I Used Deep Learning to Train a Chatbot to Talk Like Me (Sorta). At https://adeshpande3.github.io/How-I-Used-Deep-Learning-to-Train-a-Chatbot-to-Talk-Like-Me.

Desiati, M. (2017). Roma, 'TorPigna', città dalle mille etnie: Una periferia nel cuore d'Europa. *La repubblica*. At https://roma.repubblica.it/cronaca/2017/01/06/news/roma_torpignattara_citta_dalle_mille_etnie_una_periferia_nel_cuore_d_europa-155496627.

Desole, M. (2020). Bias and Diversity in Artificial Intelligence – the European Approach: The Different Roots of Bias and How Diversity Can Help in Overcoming It. *The Lab's Quarterly*, 22(2), 129–41.

DiMaggio, P. (1987). Classification in Art. *American Sociological Review*, 52(4), 440–55.

Bibliography 165

Dourish, P. (2016). Algorithms and Their Others: Algorithmic Culture in Context. *Big Data & Society*, 3(2). At https://doi.org/10.1177/2053951716665128.

Dreyfus, H.L. (1972). *What Computers Can't Do*. Harper & Row.

Dua, D. and Graff, C. (2019). UCI Machine Learning Repository. At http://archive.ics.uci.edu/ml.

Dunn, J. (2016). Introducing FBLearner Flow: Facebook's AI Backbone. *Facebook Engineering*, 9 May. At https://code.facebook.com/posts/1072626246134461/introducing-fblearner-flow-facebook-s-aibackbone.

Dwoskin, E. (2018). 'I'm Google's Automated Booking Service.' Why Duplex Is Now Introducing Itself as a Robot Assistant. *Washington Post*, 27 June. At https://www.washingtonpost.com/technology/2018/06/27/heres-why-googles-new-ai-assistant-tells-you-its-robot-even-if-it-sounds-human.

Dyer, R. (1999). Making 'White' People White. In D. MacKenzie & J. Wajcman (eds.), *The Social Shaping of Technology*. Open University Press, pp. 269–90.

Eco, U. (1964). *Apocalittici e integrati: Comunicazioni di massa e teorie della cultura di massa*. Bompiani.

Esposito, E. (2017). Artificial Communication? The Production of Contingency by Algorithms. *Zeitschrift für Soziologie*, 46(4), 249–65.

Eubanks, V. (2018). *Automating Inequality: How High-Tech Tools Profile, Police, and Punish the Poor*. St. Martin's Press.

Fields, C. (1987). Human–Computer Interaction: A Critical Synthesis. *Social Epistemology*, 1(1), 5–25.

Fjelland, R. (2020). Why General Artificial Intelligence Will Not Be Realized. *Humanities and Social Sciences Communications*, 7(1), 1–9.

Floridi, L. (2020). AI and Its New Winter: From Myths to Realities. *Philosophy & Technology*, 33(1), 1–3.

Floridi, L., Cowls, J., Beltrametti, M., Chatila, R., Chazerand, P., Dignum, V., Luetge, C., Madelin, R., Pagallo, U., Rossi, F., Schafer, B., Valcke, P. & Vayena, E. (2018). AI4People – An Ethical Framework for a Good AI Society: Opportunities, Risks, Principles, and Recommendations. *Minds and Machines*, 28(4), 689–707.

Floridi, L. & Sanders, J.W. (2004). On the Morality of Artificial Agents. *Minds and Machines*, 14(3), 349–79.

Fourcade, M. & Johns, F. (2020). Loops, Ladders and Links: The Recursivity of Social and Machine Learning. *Theory and Society*. At https://doi: 10.1007/s11186-020-09409-x.

Frank, M.R., Wang, D., Cebrian, M. & Rahwan, I. (2019). The

Evolution of Citation Graphs in Artificial Intelligence Research. *Nature Machine Intelligence, 1*(2), 79–85.

Friedler, S.A., Scheidegger, C. & Venkatasubramanian, S. (2016). On the (Im)possibility of Fairness [preprint]. At https://arxiv.org/abs/1609.07236.

Friedman, B. & Nissenbaum, H. (1996). Bias in Computer Systems. *ACM Transactions on Information Systems, 14*(3), 330–47.

Friedman, S., Savage, M., Hanquinet, L. & Miles, A. (2015). Cultural Sociology and New Forms of Distinction. *Poetics, 53*, 1–8.

Fuchs, D.J. (2018). The Dangers of Human-Like Bias in Machine-Learning Algorithms. *Missouri S&T's Peer to Peer, 2*(1). At https://scholarsmine.mst.edu/peer2peer/vol2/iss1/1.

Galeotti, M. (2018). Discriminazione e algoritmi: Incontri e scontri tra diverse idee di fairness. *The Lab's Quarterly, 22*(4), 73–95.

Gandini, A. (2020). Digital Labour: An Empty Signifier? *Media, Culture & Society*. At https://doi.org/10.1177/0163443720948018.

Garun, N. (2019). One Year Later, Restaurants Are Still Confused by Google Duplex. *The Verge*, 9 May. At https://www.theverge.com/2019/5/9/18538194/google-duplex-ai-restaurants-experiences-review-robocalls.

Gebru, T., Krause, J., Wang, Y., Chen, D., Deng, J., Aiden, E.L. & Fei-Fei, L. (2017). Using Deep Learning and Google Street View to Estimate the Demographic Makeup of Neighborhoods across the United States. *Proceedings of the National Academy of Sciences, 114*(50), 13108–13.

Geiger, R.S. (2017). Beyond Opening Up the Black Box: Investigating the Role of Algorithmic Systems in Wikipedian Organizational Culture. *Big Data & Society*. At https://doi.org/10.1177/2053951717730735.

Gerlitz, C. & Helmond, A. (2013). The Like Economy: Social Buttons and the Data-Intensive Web. *New Media & Society, 15*(8), 1348–65.

Giddens, A. (1984). *The Constitution of Society*. Polity.

Giglietto, F., Righetti, N., Rossi, L. & Marino, G. (2020). It Takes a Village to Manipulate the Media: Coordinated Link Sharing Behavior during 2018 and 2019 Italian Elections. *Information, Communication & Society, 23*(6), 867–91.

Gillespie, T. (2010). The Politics of 'Platforms'. *New Media & Society, 12*(3), 347–64.

Gillespie, T. (2014). The Relevance of Algorithms. In T. Gillespie, P.J. Boczkowski, K.A. Foot (eds.), *Media Technologies: Essays on Communication, Materiality, and Society*. MIT Press, pp. 167–93.

Gillespie, T. (2016). Algorithm. In B. Peters (ed.), *Digital Keywords*. Princeton University Press, pp. 18–30.

Gillespie, T. (2018). *Custodians of the Internet: Platforms, Content Moderation, and the Hidden Decisions that Shape Social Media.* Yale University Press.

Gillespie, T. & Seaver, N. (2016). Critical Algorithm Studies: A Reading List. *The Social Media Collective*, 15 December. At https:// social mediacollective.org/reading-lists/critical-algorithm-studies.

Goffman, E. (1983). The Interaction Order. *American Sociological Review 48*(1), 1–17.

Goldberg, A., Hannan, M.T. & Kovács, B. (2016). What Does It Mean to Span Cultural Boundaries? Variety and Atypicality in Cultural Consumption. *American Sociological Review, 81*(2), 215–41.

Gomez-Uribe, C.A. & Hunt, N. (2015). The Netflix Recommender System: Algorithms, Business Value, and Innovation. *ACM Transactions on Management Information Systems, 6*(4), 1–13.

Google (2018). Learn About the Latest Product and Platform Innovations at Google in a Keynote Led by Sundar Pichai [Video]. 8 May. At https://events.google.com/io2018/schedule/ ?section=may-8&sid=9c52752e-9a83-4c87-9a3e-46f409a16578.

GPT-3 (2020). A Robot Wrote This Entire Article: Are You Scared Yet, Human? *Guardian*, 8 September. At https://www.theguardian. com/commentisfree/2020/sep/08/robot-wrote-this-article-gpt-3.

Gran, A.B., Booth, P. & Bucher, T. (2020). To Be or Not to Be Algorithm Aware: A Question of a New Digital Divide? *Information, Communication & Society*. At https://doi.org/10.1 080/1369118X.2020.1736124.

Greene, D., Hoffmann, A.L. & Stark, L. (2019). Better, Nicer, Clearer, Fairer: A Critical Assessment of the Movement for Ethical Artificial Intelligence and Machine Learning. *Proceedings of the 52nd Hawaii International Conference on System Sciences*, pp. 2122–31. At http://hdl.handle.net/10125/59651.

Guardian (2020). Inbuilt Biases and the Problem of Algorithms. Letters. *Guardian*, 17 August. At https://www.theguardian.com/ education/2020/aug/17/inbuilt-biases-and-the-problem-of-algorithms.

Guhin, J., Calarco, J.M. & Miller-Idriss, C. (2020). Whatever Happened to Socialization? [preprint]. At https://osf.io/preprints/ socarxiv/zp2wy/download.

Hakim, C. (2010). Erotic Capital. *European Sociological Review, 26*(5), 499–518.

Halfaker, A., Geiger, R.S., Morgan, J.T., Sarabadani, A. & Wight, A. (2018). *ORES: Facilitating Re-mediation of Wikipedia's Socio-Technical Problems*. Working Paper. Wikimedia Research. At https://meta.wikimedia.org/wiki/Research:ORES:_Facilitating_re-mediation_of_Wikipedia%27s_socio-technical_problems.

Hallinan, B. & Striphas, T. (2016). Recommended for You: The Netflix Prize and the Production of Algorithmic Culture. *New Media & Society*, *18*(1), 117–37.

Hammersley, M. (2017). On the Role of Values in Social Research: Weber Vindicated? *Sociological Research Online*, *22*(1), 130–41.

Hang, D.T.D. (2018). Dataselfie.it. At https://dataselfie.it/#.

Hardesty, L. (2019). The History of Amazon's Recommendation Algorithm. *Amazon Science*, 22 November. At https://www.amazon. science/the-history-of-amazons-recommendation-algorithm.

Hardt, M., Price, E. & Srebro, N. (2016). Equality of Opportunity in Supervised Learning. *Advances in Neural Information Processing Systems*, *29*, 3315–23.

Hargittai, E. & Micheli, M. (2019). Internet Skills and Why They Matter. In M. Graham, W.H. Dutton (eds.), *Society and the Internet: How Networks of Information and Communication Are Changing Our Lives*. Oxford University Press, pp. 109–24.

Hargreaves, E., Agosti, C., Menasché, D., Neglia, G., Reiffers-Masson, A. & Altman, E. (2018). Biases in the Facebook News Feed: A Case Study on the Italian Elections. *Proceedings of the 2018 IEEE/ACM International Conference on Advances in Social Networks Analysis and Mining (ASONAM)*, pp. 806–12. At https://doi.org/10.1109/ASONAM.2018.8508659.

Harrison, O. (2018). Machine Learning Basics with the K-Nearest Neighbors Algorithm. *Towards Data Science*, 10 September. At https://towardsdatascience.com/machine-learning-basics-with-the-k-nearest-neighbors-algorithm-6a6e71d01761.

Hayles, N.K. (2005). *My Mother Was a Computer: Digital Subjects and Literary Texts*. Chicago University Press.

Helmond, A. (2015). The Platformization of the Web: Making Web Data Platform Ready. *Social Media + Society*, *1*(2). At https://doi.org/10.1177/2056305115603080.

Helmond, A., Nieborg, D.B. & van der Vlist, F.N. (2019). Facebook's Evolution: Development of a Platform-as-Infrastructure. *Internet Histories*, *3*(2), 123–46.

Higginbotham, S. (2016). Inside Facebook's Biggest Artificial Intelligence Project Ever. *Fortune*, 13 April. At http://fortune. com/facebook-machine-learning.

Hildt, E. (2019). Artificial Intelligence: Does Consciousness Matter? *Frontiers in Psychology*, *10*. At https://doi.org/10.3389/fpsyg.2019.01535.

Hoffmann, A.L. (2019). Where Fairness Fails: Data, Algorithms, and the Limits of Antidiscrimination Discourse. *Information, Communication & Society*, 22(7), 900–15.

Hofstra, B., Corten, R., Van Tubergen, F. & Ellison, N.B. (2017). Sources of Segregation in Social Networks: A Novel Approach Using Facebook. *American Sociological Review*, 82(3), 625–56.

Iaconesi, S. & Persico, O. (2019). A Torpignattara c'è un'intelligenza artificiale di quartiere — si chiama IAQOS. *Che fare*, 30 May. At https://www.che-fare.com/iaqos-intelligenza-artificiale-torpignattara.

IAQOS (2019). Intelligenza Artificiale di Quartiere Open Source. At https://iaqos.online/site.

IFPI (2018). *Music Consumer Insight Report 2018*. International Federation of the Phonographic Industry. At https://www.ifpi.org/wp-content/uploads/2020/07/091018_Music-Consumer-Insight-Report-2018.pdf.

Instagram (2016). See Posts You Care About First in Your Feed. 15 March. At https://about.instagram.com/blog/announcements/see-posts-you-care-about-first-in-your-feed.

Irani, L. (2015). The Cultural Work of Microwork. *New Media & Society*, 17(5), 720–39.

IWS (2020). Internet World Stats. At https://www.internetworld-stats.com.

Jacobsen, B.N. (2020). Algorithms and the Narration of Past Selves. *Information, Communication & Society*. At https://doi.org/10.1080/1369118X.2020.1834603.

Jarness, V. (2015). Modes of Consumption: From 'What' to 'How' in Cultural Stratification Research. *Poetics*, 53, 65–79.

Jenkins, R. (1993). *Pierre Bourdieu*. Routledge.

Jiang, H. & Nachum, O. (2020). Identifying and Correcting Label Bias in Machine Learning. *Proceedings of the 23rd International Conference on Artificial Intelligence and Statistics* (AISTATS), pp. 713–23. At http://proceedings.mlr.press/v108.

Jiang, R., Chiappa, S., Lattimore, T., György, A. & Kohli, P. (2019). Degenerate Feedback Loops in Recommender Systems. *Proceedings of the 2019 AAAI/ACM Conference on AI, Ethics, and Society*, pp. 383–90. At https://doi.org/10.1145/3306618.3314288.

Just, N. & Latzer, M. (2017). Governance by Algorithms: Reality Construction by Algorithmic Selection on the Internet. *Media, Culture & Society*, 39(2), 238–58.

Karkare, P. (2019). Neural Style Transfer: Using Deep Learning to Generate Art. *Medium*, 7 September. At https://medium.com/x8-the-ai-community/neural-style-transfer-using-deep-learning-to-generate-art-651d9ccf740c.

Karppi, T. & Crawford, K. (2016). Social Media, Financial

Algorithms and the Hack Crash. *Theory, Culture & Society*, *33*(1), 73–92.

Kaufmann, M., Egbert, S., & Leese, M. (2019). Predictive Policing and the Politics of Patterns. *The British Journal of Criminology*, *59*(3), 674–92.

Kelleher, J.D. (2019). *Deep Learning*. MIT Press.

Kellogg, K.C., Valentine, M.A. & Christin, A. (2020). Algorithms at Work: The New Contested Terrain of Control. *Academy of Management Annals*, *14*(1), 366–410.

Kennedy, S. (2017). Potentially Deadly Bomb Ingredients Are 'Frequently Bought Together' on Amazon. *Channel 4*, 18 September. At https://www.channel4.com/news/potentially-deadly-bomb-ingredients-on-amazon.

Kim, T.W., Donaldson, T. & Hooker, J. (2018). Mimetic vs Anchored Value Alignment in Artificial Intelligence [preprint]. At http://arxiv.org/abs/1810.11116.

King, A. (2000). Thinking with Bourdieu against Bourdieu: A 'Practical' Critique of the Habitus. *Sociological Theory*, *18*(3), 417–33.

Kirchner, C. & Mohr, J. W. (2010). Meanings and Relations: An Introduction to the Study of Language, Discourse and Networks. *Poetics*, *38*(6), 555–66.

Kitchin, R. (2017). Thinking Critically About and Researching Algorithms. *Information, Communication & Society*, *20*(1), 14–29.

Kitchin, R. & Dodge, M. (2011). *Code/Space: Software and Everyday Life*. MIT Press.

Klawitter, E. & Hargittai, E. (2018). 'It's Like Learning a Whole Other Language': The Role of Algorithmic Skills in the Curation of Creative Goods. *International Journal of Communication*, *2018*(12), 3490–510.

Knorr Cetina, K. (2009). The Synthetic Situation: Interactionism for a Global World. *Symbolic Interaction*, *32*(1), 61–87.

König, R. & Rasch, M. (2014). *Society of the Query Reader: Reflections on Web Search*. Institute of Network Cultures.

Konstan, J.A. & Riedl, J. (2012). Recommender Systems: From Algorithms to User Experience. *User Modeling and User-Adapted Interaction*, *22*(1–2), 101–23.

Kozlowski, A.C., Taddy, M. & Evans, J.A. (2019). The Geometry of Culture: Analyzing the Meanings of Class through Word Embeddings. *American Sociological Review*, *84*(5), 905–49.

Krafcik, J. (2020). Waymo is Opening Its Fully Driverless Service to the General Public in Phoenix. 8 October. At https://blog.waymo.com/2020/10/waymo-is-opening-its-fully-driverless.html.

Krasmann, S. (2020). The Logic of the Surface: On the Epistemology of Algorithms in Times of Big Data. *Information, Communication & Society*, 23(14), 2096–109.

Krippendorff, K. (2013). *Content Analysis: An Introduction to Its Methodology*. Sage.

La Quadrature du Net (2020). Police Racism: Net's Giants Are Pretending to Stop Facial Recognition. 16 October. At https://www.laquadrature.net/en/2020/10/16/police-racism-nets-giants-are-pretending-to-stop-facial-recognition.

Lahire, B. (2004). *La culture des individus: Dissonances culturelles et distinction de soi*. La Découverte.

Lahire, B. (2019). Sociological Biography and Socialisation Process: A Dispositionalist-Contextualist Conception. *Contemporary Social Science*, 14(3–4), 379–93.

Lamont, M. & Molnár, V. (2002). The Study of Boundaries in the Social Sciences. *Annual Review of Sociology*, 28(1), 167–95.

Larson, J., Mattu, S., Kirchner, L. & Angwin, J. (2016). How We Analyzed the COMPAS Recidivism Algorithm. *Propublica*, 23 May. At https://www.propublica.org/article/how-we-analyzed-the-compas-recidivism-algorithm.

Lash, S. (2007). Power after Hegemony: Cultural Studies in Mutation? *Theory, Culture & Society*, 24(3), 55–78.

Latour, B. (1992). Where Are the Missing Masses? In W. Bijker & J. Law (eds.), *Shaping Technology/Building Society: Studies in Sociotechnical Change*. MIT Press, pp. 225–58.

Latour, B. (2005). *Reassembling the Social: An Introduction to Actor-Network-Theory*. Oxford University Press.

Latour, B., Jensen, P., Venturini, T., Grauwin, S. & Boullier, D. (2012). 'The Whole Is Always Smaller than Its Parts': A Digital Test of Gabriel Tarde's Monads. *The British Journal of Sociology*, 63(4), 590–615.

Latour, B. & Woolgar, S. (1986). *Laboratory Life: The Construction of Scientific Facts*. Princeton University Press.

Law, J. (1990). Introduction: Monsters, Machines and Sociotechnical Relations. *The Sociological Review*, 38(1 suppl), 1–23.

Lazarsfeld, P.F., Berelson, B. & Gaudet, H. (1944). *The People's Choice: How the Voter Makes Up His Mind in a Presidential Campaign*. Duell, Sloan & Pearce.

Leavy, S. (2018). Gender Bias in Artificial Intelligence: The Need for Diversity and Gender Theory in Machine Learning. *Proceedings of the 1st International Workshop on Gender Equality in Software Engineering*, pp. 14–16. At https://doi.org/10.1145/3195570.3195580.

Lelo, K., Monni, S. & Tomassi, F. (2019). *Le mappe della disuguaglianza. Una geografia sociale metropolitana*. Donzelli Editore.

Lenat, D.B. (1989). When Will Machines Learn? *Machine Learning*, *4*, 255–7.

Lessig, L. (2006). *Code (Version 2.0)*. Basic Books.

Leviathan, Y., and Matias, Y. (2018). Google Duplex: An AI System for Accomplishing Real-World Tasks over the Phone. *Google AI Blog*. 8 May. At https://ai.googleblog.com/2018/05/duplex-ai-system-for-natural-conversation.html.

Levina, N. & Arriaga, M. (2014). Distinction and Status Production on User-Generated Content Platforms: Using Bourdieu's Theory of Cultural Production to Understand Social Dynamics in Online Fields. *Information Systems Research*, *25*(3), 468–88.

Light, B., Burgess, J. & Duguay, S. (2018). The Walkthrough Method: An Approach to the Study of Apps. *New Media & Society*, *20*(3), 881–900.

Lizardo, O. (2004). The Cognitive Origins of Bourdieu's Habitus. *Journal for the Theory of Social Behaviour*, *34*(4), 375–401.

Lizardo, O. (2013). Habitus. In B. Kaldis (ed.), *Encyclopedia of Philosophy and the Social Sciences*, Vol. 1. Sage, pp. 405–7.

Lizardo, O. (2017). Improving Cultural Analysis: Considering Personal Culture in Its Declarative and Nondeclarative Modes. *American Sociological Review*, *82*(1), 88–115.

Lupton, D. (2020). The Internet of Things: Social Dimensions. *Sociology Compass*, *14*(4). At https://doi.org/10.1111/soc4.12770.

Lutz, C. (2019). Digital Inequalities in the Age of Artificial Intelligence and Big Data. *Human Behavior and Emerging Technologies*, *1*(2), 141–8.

MacCormick, J. (2012). *9 Algorithms that Changed the Future: The Ingenious Ideas that Drive Today's Computers*. Princeton University Press.

McKelvey, F. (2018). *Internet Daemons: Digital Communications Possessed*. University of Minnesota Press.

Mackenzie, A. (2006). *Cutting Code: Software and Sociality*. Peter Lang.

Mackenzie, A. (2015). The Production of Prediction: What Does Machine Learning Want? *European Journal of Cultural Studies*, *18*(4–5), 429–45.

Mackenzie, A. (2018). Personalization and Probabilities: Impersonal Propensities in Online Grocery Shopping. *Big Data & Society*, *5*(1). At https://doi.org/10.1177/2053951718778310.

Mackenzie, A. (2019). From API to AI: Platforms and Their Opacities. *Information, Communication & Society*, *22*(13), 1989–2006.

MacKenzie, D. (1996). *Knowing Machines: Essays on Technological Change*. MIT Press.

MacKenzie, D. (2018). Material Signals: A Historical Sociology of High-Frequency Trading. *American Journal of Sociology*, 123(6), 1635–83.

MacKenzie, D. (2019). How Algorithms Interact: Goffman's 'Interaction Order' in Automated Trading. *Theory, Culture & Society*, 36(2), 39–59.

MacKenzie, D. & Wajcman, J. (1999). *The Social Shaping of Technology*. Open University Press.

Manovich, L. (2002). *The Language of New Media*. MIT Press.

Marcus, G.E. (1995). Ethnography in/of the World System: The Emergence of Multi-Sited Ethnography. *Annual Review of Anthropology*, 24, 95–117.

Marres, N. & Gerlitz, C. (2016). Interface Methods: Renegotiating Relations between Digital Social Research, STS and Sociology. *The Sociological Review*, 64(1), 21–46.

Martin, J.L. & George, M. (2006). Theories of Sexual Stratification: Toward an Analytics of the Sexual Field and a Theory of Sexual Capital. *Sociological Theory*, 24(2), 107–32.

Martin, K. (2019). Ethical Implications and Accountability of Algorithms. *Journal of Business Ethics*, 160(4), 835–50.

Mayer-Schoenberger, V. & Cukier, K. (2013). *Big Data. A Revolution that Will Transform How We Live, Work, and Think*. John Murray.

Mellet, K. & Beauvisage, T. (2020). Cookie Monsters: Anatomy of a Digital Market Infrastructure. *Consumption, Markets & Culture*, 23(2), 110–29.

Mercer, J.R. (1978). Test 'Validity', 'Bias', and 'Fairness': An Analysis from the Perspective of the Sociology of Knowledge. *Interchange*, 9(1), 1–16.

Micheli, M., Lutz, C. & Moritz, B. (2018). Digital Footprints: An Emerging Dimension of Digital Inequality. *Journal of Information, Communication and Ethics in Society*, 16(3), 242–51.

Mihelj, S., Leguina, A. & Downey, J. (2019). Culture Is Digital: Cultural Participation, Diversity and the Digital Divide. *New Media & Society*, 21(7), 1465–85.

Milan, S. (2015). When Algorithms Shape Collective Action: Social Media and the Dynamics of Cloud Protesting. *Social Media + Society*, 1(2). At https://doi.org/10.1177/2056305115622481.

Millière, R. (2020). Welcome to the Next Level of Bullshit: The Language Algorithm GPT-3 Continues Our Descent into a Post-Truth World. *Nautilus*, 9 September. At http://nautil.us/issue/89/the-dark-side/welcome-to-the-next-level-of-bullshit.

Mills, C.W. (1959). *The Sociological Imagination*. Oxford University Press.

Mills, M.C. & Tropf, F. C. (2020). Sociology, Genetics, and the Coming of Age of Sociogenomics. *Annual Review of Sociology*, 46(1), 553–81.

Morris, J.W. (2015). Curation by Code: Infomediaries and the Data Mining of Taste. *European Journal of Cultural Studies*, 18(4–5), 446–63.

Mühlhoff, R. (2020). Human-Aided Artificial Intelligence: Or, How to Run Large Computations in Human Brains? Toward a Media Sociology of Machine Learning. *New Media & Society*, 22(10), 1868–84.

Mukerji, C. (2014). The Cultural Power of Tacit Knowledge: Inarticulacy and Bourdieu's Habitus. *American Journal of Cultural Sociology*, 2(3), 348–75.

Mullainathan, S. (2019). Biased Algorithms Are Easier to Fix than Biased People. *New York Times*, 6 December. At https://www.nytimes.com/2019/12/06/business/algorithm-bias-fix.html.

Müller, M. (2015). Assemblages and Actor-Networks: Rethinking Socio-Material Power, Politics and Space. *Geography Compass*, 9(1), 27–41.

Napoli, P.M. & Obar, J.A. (2014). The Emerging Mobile Internet Underclass: A Critique of Mobile Internet Access. *The Information Society*, 30(5), 323–34.

Natale, S. & Ballatore, A. (2020). Imagining the Thinking Machine: Technological Myths and the Rise of Artificial Intelligence. *Convergence: The International Journal of Research into New Media Technologies*, 26(1), 3–18.

Newman, N., Fletcher, R., Levy, D.A.L. & Nielsen, R.K. (2016). *Reuters Institute Digital News Report 2016*. At http://media.digitalnewsreport.org/wp-content/uploads/2018/11/Digital-News-Report-2016.pdf?x11311.

Neyland, D. (2019). *The Everyday Life of an Algorithm*. Springer International.

Noble, S.U. (2018). *Algorithms of Oppression: How Search Engines Reinforce Racism*. NYU Press.

Nunes, M. (1997). What Space Is Cyberspace? The Internet and Virtuality. In D. Holmes (ed.), *Virtual Politics*. Sage, pp. 163–78.

Olteanu, A., Castillo, C., Diaz, F. & Kıcıman, E. (2019). Social Data: Biases, Methodological Pitfalls, and Ethical Boundaries. *Frontiers in Big Data*, 2(13). At https://doi.org/10.3389/fdata.2019.00013.

O'Neil, C. (2016). *Weapons of Math Destruction: How Big Data Increases Inequality and Threatens Democracy*. Crown.

Orlikowski, W.J. (1992). The Duality of Technology: Rethinking the Concept of Technology in Organizations. *Organization Science*, 3(3), 398–427.

Orlikowski, W.J. (2007). Sociomaterial Practices: Exploring Technology at Work. *Organization Studies, 28*(9), 1435–48.

Orton-Johnson, K. & Prior, N. (2013). *Digital Sociology: Critical Perspectives*. Palgrave Macmillan.

Page, L., Brin, S., Motwani, R., and Winograd, T. (1999). The PageRank Citation Ranking: Bringing Order to the Web. *Stanford InfoLab*. At http://ilpubs.stanford.edu:8090/422.

Pardo-Guerra, J.P. (2010). Creating Flows of Interpersonal Bits: The Automation of the London Stock Exchange, 1955–90. *Economy and Society, 39*(1), 84–109.

Pariser, E. (2011). *The Filter Bubble: How the New Personalized Web Is Changing What We Read and How We Think*. Penguin.

Pasquale, F. (2015). *The Black Box Society*. Harvard University Press.

Pasquale, F. (2020). 'Machines Set Loose to Slaughter': The Dangerous Rise of Military AI. *Guardian*, 15 October. At https://www.theguardian.com/news/2020/oct/15/dangerous-rise-of-military-ai-drone-swarm-autonomous-weapons.

Pasquinelli, M. (2017). Machines that Morph Logic: Neural Networks and the Distorted Automation of Intelligence as Statistical Inference. *Glass Bead Journal*. At https://www.glass-bead.org/wp-content/uploads/GB_Site-1_Matteo-Pasquinelli_Eng.pdf.

Pasquinelli, M. (2018). Metadata Society. In R. Braidotti & M. Hlavajova (eds.), *Posthuman Glossary*. Bloomsbury, pp. 253–6.

Pedreschi, D., Giannotti, F., Guidotti, R., Monreale, A., Pappalardo, L., Ruggieri, S. & Turini, F. (2018). Open the Black Box: Data-Driven Explanation of Black Box Decision Systems [preprint]. At http://arxiv.org/abs/1806.09936.

Pine II, J.B., Peppers, D. & Rogers, M. (1995). Do You Want to Keep Your Customers Forever? *Harvard Business Review*, March–April, 103–14.

Plantin, J.C., Lagoze, C., Edwards, P.N. & Sandvig, C. (2018). Infrastructure Studies Meet Platform Studies in the Age of Google and Facebook. *New Media & Society, 20*(1), 293–310.

Popper, K.R. (1990) *A World of Propensities*. Thoemmes Continuum.

Prey, R. (2018). Nothing Personal: Algorithmic Individuation on Music Streaming Platforms. *Media, Culture & Society, 40*(7), 1086–100.

Procacci, G. & Szakolczai, A. (2003). *La scoperta della società. Alle origini della sociologia*. Carocci.

Ragnedda, M. & Ruiu, M.L. (2020). *Digital Capital: A Bourdieusian Perspective on the Digital Divide*. Emerald Group.

Rahwan, I., Cebrian, M., Obradovich, N., Bongard, J., Bonnefon,

J.F., Breazeal, C., Crandall, J.W., Christakis, N.A., Couzin, I.D., Jackson, M.O., Jennings, N.R., Kamar, E., Kloumann, I.M., Larochelle, H., Lazer, D., McElreath, R., Mislove, A., Parkes, D.C., Pentland, A. 'Sandy', ... Wellman, M. (2019). Machine Behaviour. *Nature*, *568*(7753), 477–86.

Ranson, G. & Reeves, W.J. (1996). Gender, Earnings, and Proportions of Women: Lessons from a High-Tech Occupation. *Gender & Society*, *10*(2), 168–84.

Reviglio, U. & Agosti, C. (2020). Thinking Outside the Black-Box: The Case for 'Algorithmic Sovereignty' in Social Media. *Social Media + Society*, *6*(2). At https://doi.org/10.1177/2056305120915613.

Rieder, B. (2017). Scrutinizing an Algorithmic Technique: The Bayes Classifier as Interested Reading of Reality. *Information, Communication & Society*, *20*(1), 100–17.

Rieder, B. (2020). *Engines of Order: A Mechanology of Algorithmic Techniques*. Amsterdam University Press. At https://library.oapen.org/handle/20.500.12657/39371.

Rieder, B., Matamoros-Fernández, A. & Coromina, Ò. (2018). From Ranking Algorithms to 'Ranking Cultures': Investigating the Modulation of Visibility in YouTube Search Results. *Convergence*, *24*(1), 50–68.

Rogers, R. (2013). *Digital Methods*. MIT Press.

Roio, D. (2018). *Algorithmic Sovereignty*. Unpublished PhD thesis, University of Plymouth.

Rokka, J. & Airoldi, M. (2018). Cambridge Analytica's 'Secret' Psychographic Tool Is a Ghost from the Past. *The Conversation*, 2 April. At https://theconversation.com/cambridge-analyticas-secret-psychographic-tool-is-a-ghost-from-the-past-94143.

Rolle, M. (2019). The Biases We Feed to Tinder Algorithms. *Diggit Magazine*, 25 February. At https://www.diggitmagazine.com/articles/biases-we-feed-tinder-algorithms.

Rose, J. & Jones, M. (2005). The Double Dance of Agency: A Socio-Theoretic Account of How Machines and Humans Interact. *Systems, Signs & Actions*, *1*(1), 19–37.

Roselli, D., Matthews, J. & Talagala, N. (2019). Managing Bias in AI. (Conference presentation). 2019 World Wide Web Conference, pp. 539–44. At https://doi.org/10.1145/3308560.3317590.

Rosenblat, A. & Stark, L. (2016). Algorithmic Labor and Information Asymmetries: A Case Study of Uber's Drivers. *International Journal of Communication*, *2016*(10), 3758–84.

Rosenfeld, M.J. & Thomas, R. J. (2012). Searching for a Mate: The Rise of the Internet as a Social Intermediary. *American Sociological Review*, *77*(4), 523–47.

Roth, C., Mazières, A. & Menezes, T. (2020). Tubes and Bubbles Topological Confinement of YouTube Recommendations. *PLOS ONE, 15*(4). At https://doi.org/10.1371/journal.pone.0231703.

Ruckenstein, M. & Granroth, J. (2020). Algorithms, Advertising and the Intimacy of Surveillance. *Journal of Cultural Economy, 13*(1), 12–24.

Safra, L., Chevallier, C., Grèzes, J. & Baumard, N. (2020). Tracking Historical Changes in Trustworthiness Using Machine Learning Analyses of Facial Cues in Paintings. *Nature Communications, 11*(1), 1–7.

Salganik, M.J. (2018). *Bit by Bit: Social Research in the Digital Age*. Princeton University Press.

Saracino, B. (2018). *I giochi, le stelle e l'uomo: studio sociologico della curva normale*. Mimesis.

Schirato, T. & Roberts, M. (2018). *Bourdieu: A Critical Introduction*. Allen & Unwin.

Schwalbe, N. & Wahl, B. (2020). Artificial Intelligence and the Future of Global Health. *The Lancet, 395*(10236), 1579–86.

Science Magazine (2018). How Researchers Are Teaching AI to Learn Like a Child. [Video]. 24 May. At https://www.youtube.com/watch?v=79zHbBuFHmw.

Sculley, D. & Cormack, G.V. (2008). Filtering Email Spam in the Presence of Noisy User Feedback. *Proceedings of the Annual International ACM/SIGIR Conference on Email and Anti-Spam*. At https://dblp.org/rec/conf/ceas/SculleyC08.html.

Seaver, N. (2017). Algorithms as Culture: Some Tactics for the Ethnography of Algorithmic Systems. *Big Data & Society, 4*(2). At https://doi.org/10.1177/2053951717738104.

Seaver, N. (2019). Captivating Algorithms: Recommender Systems as Traps. *Journal of Material Culture, 24*(4), 421–36.

Siles, I., Segura-Castillo, A., Solís, R. & Sancho, M. (2020). Folk Theories of Algorithmic Recommendations on Spotify: Enacting Data Assemblages in the Global South. *Big Data & Society*. At https://doi.org/10.1177/2053951720923377.

Silver, D. & Hassabis, D. (2017). AlphaGo Zero: Starting from Scratch. *Deep Mind*. At https://deepmind.com/blog/article/alphago-zero-starting-scratch.

Smith, B. & Linden, G. (2017). Two Decades of Recommender Systems at Amazon.com. *IEEE Internet Computing, 21*(3), 12–18. At https://doi.org/10.1109/MIC.2017.72.

Sparrow, R. (2020). Robotics Has a Race Problem. *Science, Technology & Human Values, 45*(3), 538–60.

Sterne, J. (2003). Bourdieu, Technique and Technology. *Cultural Studies, 17*(3–4), 367–89.

Sterne, J. (2016). Analog. In B. Peters (ed.), *Digital Keywords*. Princeton University Press, pp. 31–44.

Strand, M. & Lizardo, O. (2017). The Hysteresis Effect: Theorizing Mismatch in Action. *Journal for the Theory of Social Behaviour*, 47(2), 164–94.

Striphas, T. (2015). Algorithmic Culture. *European Journal of Cultural Studies*, 18(4–5), 395–412.

Summers, C.A., Smith, R.W. & Reczek, R.W. (2016). An Audience of One: Behaviorally Targeted Ads as Implied Social Labels. *Journal of Consumer Research*, 43(1), 156–78.

Sumpter, D. (2018). *Outnumbered: From Facebook and Google to Fake News and Filter-Bubbles – the Algorithms that Control Our Lives*. Bloomsbury.

Tassabehji, R., Harding, N., Lee, H. & Dominguez-Pery, C. (2021). From Female Computers to Male Computers: Or Why There Are So Few Women Writing Algorithms and Developing Software. *Human Relations*, 74(8), 1296–326.

Taylor, F. (2003). Content Analysis and Gender Stereotypes in Children's Books. *Teaching Sociology*, 31, 300–11.

Telford, T. (2019). Apple Card Algorithm Sparks Gender Bias Allegations against Goldman Sachs. *Washington Post*, 11 November. At https://www.washingtonpost.com/business/2019/11/11/apple-card-algorithm-sparks-gender-bias-allegations-against-goldman-sachs.

Thrift, N. (2005) *Knowing Capitalism*. Sage.

Tracking Exposed (2019). *Tracking Exposed Manifesto*. At https://tracking.exposed/manifesto.

Tricot, A. & Chesné, J.F. (2020). *Numérique et apprentissages scolaires: rapport de synthèse*. Cnesco.

Tsvetkova, M., García-Gavilanes, R., Floridi, L. & Yasseri, T. (2017). Even Good Bots Fight: The Case of Wikipedia. *PLOS ONE*, 12(2). At https://doi.org/10.1371/journal.pone.0171774.

Tubaro, P., Casilli, A.A. & Coville, M. (2020). The Trainer, the Verifier, the Imitator: Three Ways in which Human Platform Workers Support Artificial Intelligence. *Big Data & Society*, 7(1). At https://doi.org/10.1177/2053951720919776.

Tufekci, Z. (2015). Algorithmic Harms beyond Facebook and Google: Emergent Challenges of Computational Agency. *Colorado Technology Law Journal*, 13, 203–18.

Tufekci, Z. (2018). Opinion: YouTube, the Great Radicalizer. *New York Times*, 10 March. At https://www.nytimes.com/2018/03/10/opinion/sunday/youtube-politics-radical.html.

Turner, F. (2017). Don't Be Evil: Fred Turner on Utopias, Frontiers, and Brogrammers. *Logic*, Issue 3/Justice, 1 December. At https://logicmag.io/justice/fred-turner-dont-be-evil.

Ugander, J., Karrer, B., Backstrom, L., & Marlow, C. (2011). The Anatomy of the Facebook Social Graph [preprint]. At https://arxiv.org/abs/1111.4503.

Vaisey, S. (2009). Motivation and Justification: A Dual-Process Model of Culture in Action. *American Journal of Sociology*, *114*(6), 1675–1715.

van Dijck, J. (2013). *The Culture of Connectivity: A Critical History of Social Media*. Oxford University Press.

van Dijck, J., Poell, T. & de Waal, M. (2018). *The Platform Society: Public Values in a Connective World*. Oxford University Press.

Velkova, J. & Kaun, A. (2019). Algorithmic Resistance: Media Practices and the Politics of Repair. *Information, Communication & Society*. At https://doi.org/10.1080/1369118X.2019.1657162.

Venturini, T., Bounegru, L., Gray, J. & Rogers, R. (2018). A Reality Check(list) for Digital Methods. *New Media & Society*, *20*(11), 4195–217.

Vézina, B. & Moran, B. (2020). Artificial Intelligence and Creativity: Can Machines Write Like Jane Austen? *Creative Commons*, 10 August. At https://creativecommons.org/2020/08/10/can-machines-write-like-jane-austen.

Vincent, J. (2017). A Bot on Amazon Is Making the Best, Worst Smartphones Cases. *The Verge*, 10 July. At https://www.theverge.com/tldr/2017/7/10/15946296/amazon-bot-smartphone-cases.

Wacquant, L. (2002). *Corps et âme: carnets ethnographiques d'un apprenti boxeur*. Agone.

Watson, D. (2019). The Rhetoric and Reality of Anthropomorphism in Artificial Intelligence. *Minds and Machines*, *29*(3), 417–40.

Webster, J. (2019). Music On-Demand: A Commentary on the Changing Relationship between Music Taste, Consumption and Class in the Streaming Age. *Big Data & Society*, *6*(2). At https://doi.org/10.1177/2053951719888770.

Weinberg, J. (2020). Philosophers On GPT-3 (Updated with Replies by GPT-3). *Daily Nous*, 30 July. At http://dailynous.com/2020/07/30/philosophers-gpt-3.

Wiener, N. (1989). *The Human Use of Human Beings: Cybernetics and Society*. Free Association Books.

Williams, R. (1983). *Keywords: A Vocabulary of Culture and Society* (revised edition). Oxford University Press.

Wilson, D.C.S. (2018). Babbage among the Insurers: Big 19th-Century Data and the Public Interest. *History of the Human Sciences*, *31*(5), 129–53.

Woolgar, S. (1985). Why Not a Sociology of Machines? The Case of Sociology and Artificial Intelligence. *Sociology, 19*(4), 557–72.

Wu, S., Rizoiu, M.A. & Xie, L. (2019). Estimating Attention Flow in Online Video Networks. *Proceedings of the ACM on Human-Computer Interaction, 3*(CSCW), 1–25. At https://doi.org/10.1145/3359285.

Wu, X. & Zhang, X. (2016). Automated Inference on Criminality Using Face Images [preprint]. At https://arxiv.org/abs/1611.04135v1.

YouTube (2020). YouTube by the Numbers. At https://www.youtube.com/about/press.

Yu, H., Shen, Z., Miao, C., Leung, C., Lesser, V.R. & Yang, Q. (2018). Building Ethics into Artificial Intelligence [preprint]. At http://arXiv.org/abs/1812.02953.

Završnik, A. (2019). Algorithmic Justice: Algorithms and Big Data in Criminal Justice Settings. *European Journal of Criminology.* At https://doi.org/10.1177/1477370819876762.

Ziewitz, M. (2016). Governing Algorithms: Myth, Mess, and Methods. *Science, Technology & Human Values, 41*(1), 3–16.

Zuboff, S. (2019). *The Age of Surveillance Capitalism: The Fight for a Human Future at the New Frontier of Power.* Profile Books.

Zwick, D. & Denegri Knott, J. (2009). Manufacturing Customers: The Database as New Means of Production. *Journal of Consumer Culture, 9*(2), 221–47.

Zwick, D. & Dholakia, N. (2004). Whose Identity Is It Anyway? Consumer Representation in the Age of Database Marketing. *Journal of Macromarketing, 24*(1), 31–43.

Index